Hidden Cities
Coloring Book!

Tamara Kulish

All rights reserved. No part of this book may be distributed or reproduced in any format or by any electronic or mechanical means without the written permission from the author.

ISBN-13: 978-1986352833
ISBN-10: 1986352838

Published 2018
Copyright © 2018 Tamara Kulish
Cover design © 2017 by Tamara Kulish
Original artwork © 2015 by Tamara Kulish

Hidden Cities Coloring book!

Love the coloring craze?
This book is all about my favorite cities
and the ones which are on my Bucket List!
I've created coloring pages which are
almost like "Hidden Eye" designs!

For the Travel Buff and the Dreamer!
Challenging and Relaxing!

Here's a coloring book with hidden names of cities,
decorated with flowers and hearts
so you can sit, relax and just have fun!
There's 3 challenge levels for each city,
so your fun is extended!

All of these designs are also on Fine Art America!

http://fineartamerica.com/profiles/tamara-kulish.html
You can order any of their products and
they will custom print and ship it to you!
Imagine painting any one of these designs on a
large pre-printed gallery-wrapped canvas!

Other books available on Tamara's Amazon Author page:
https://www.amazon.com/Tamara-Kulish/e/B00IVWCAEI/

Tamara Kulish is an artist, a writer, a photographer, a jewelry maker,
a seeker and a life voyager.

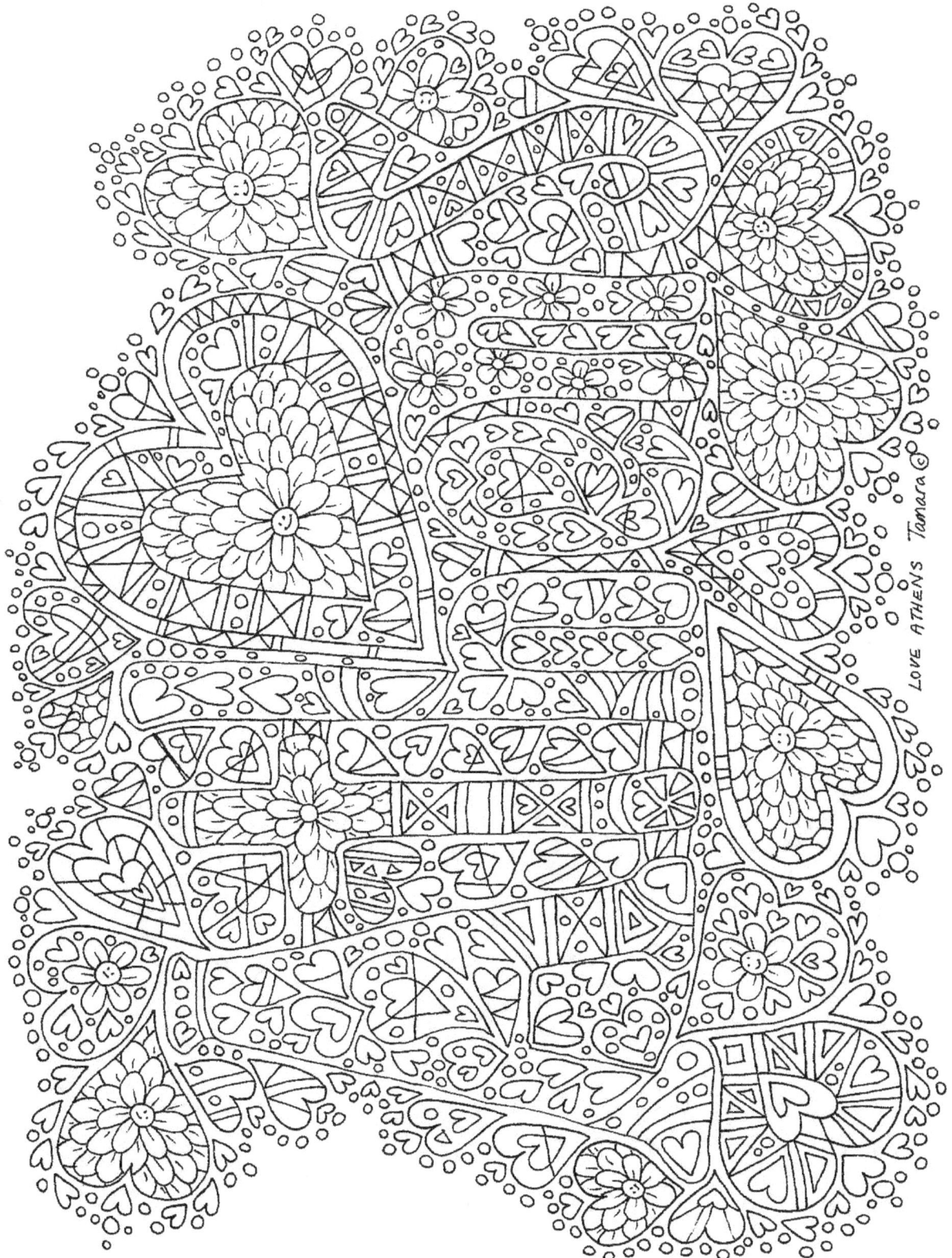

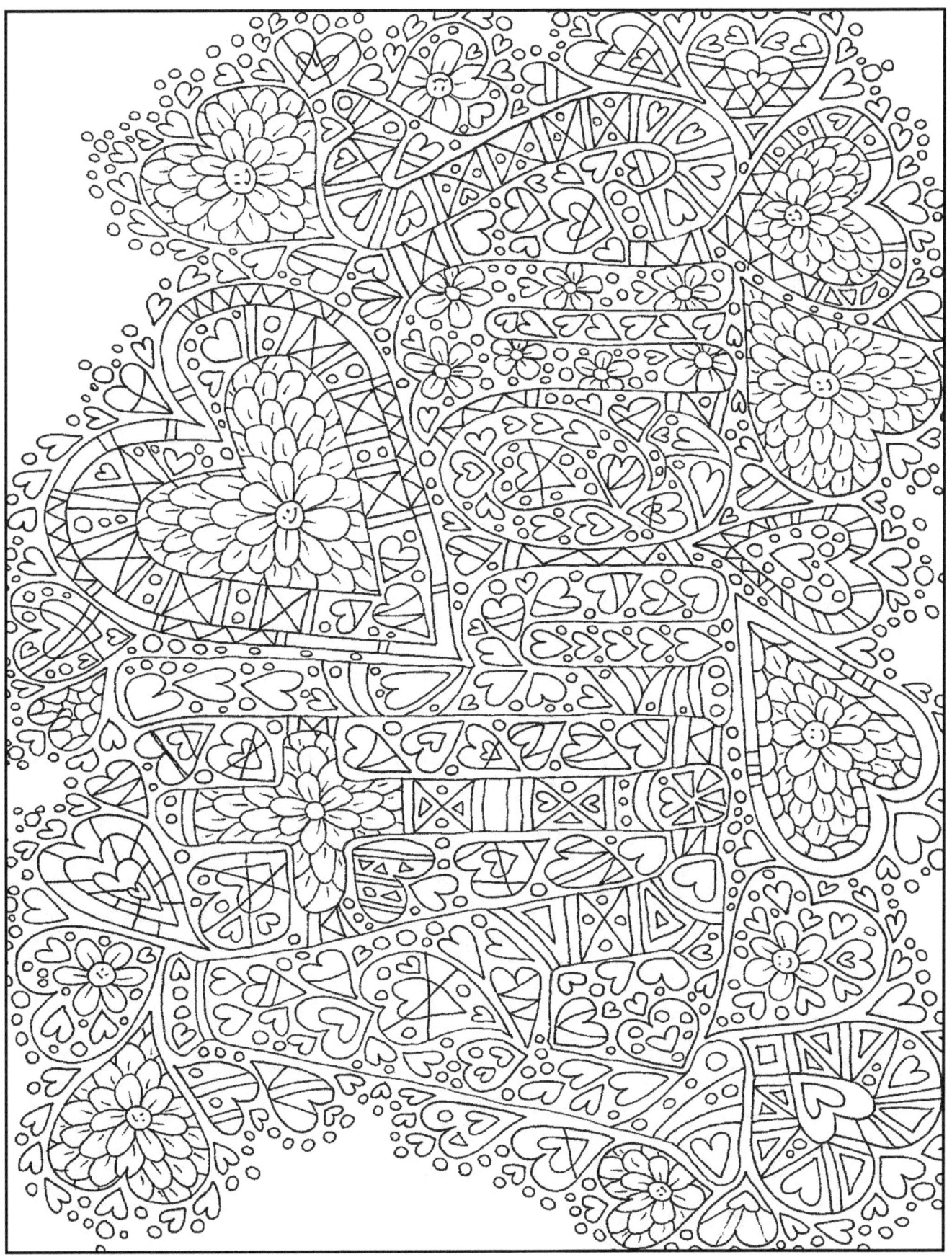

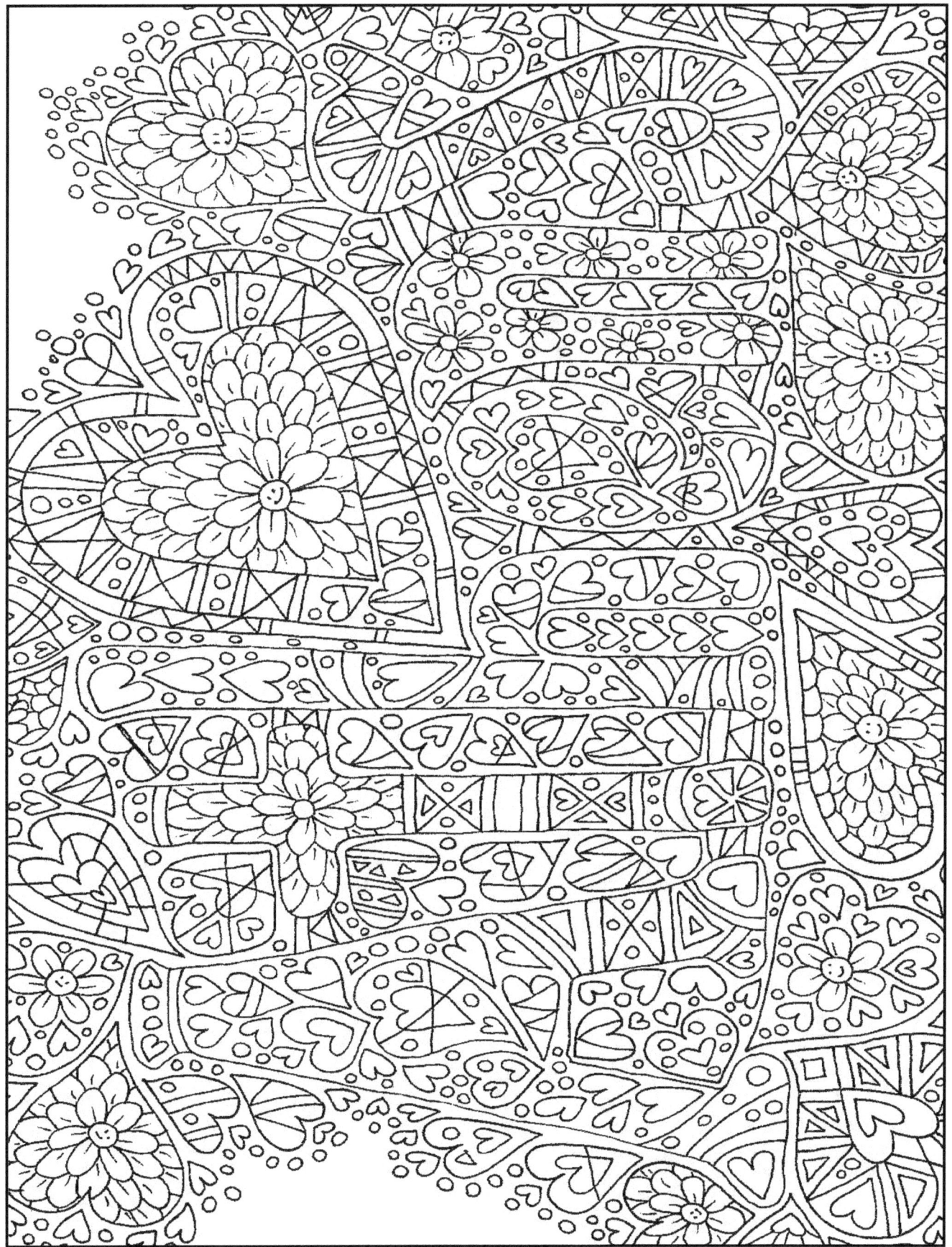

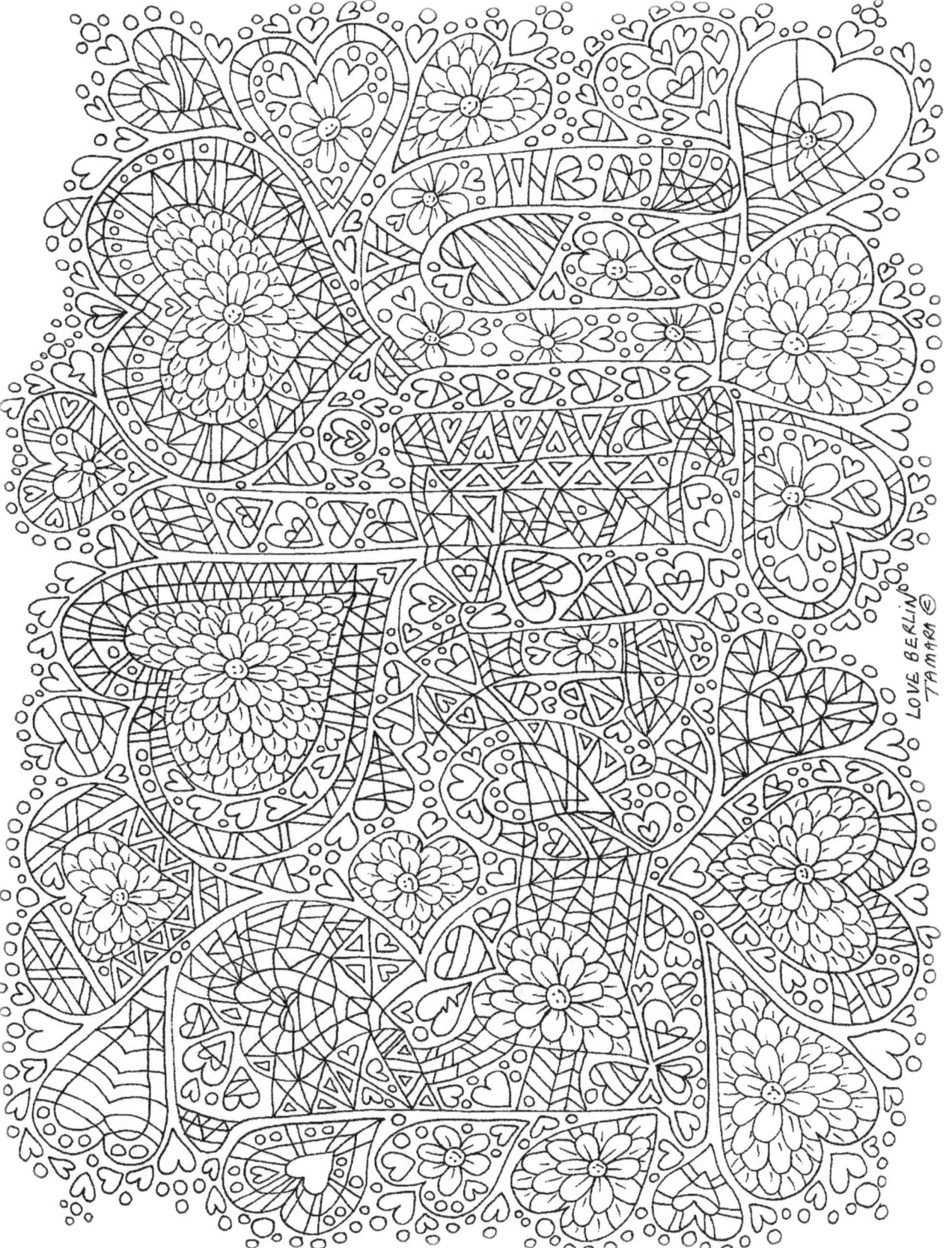

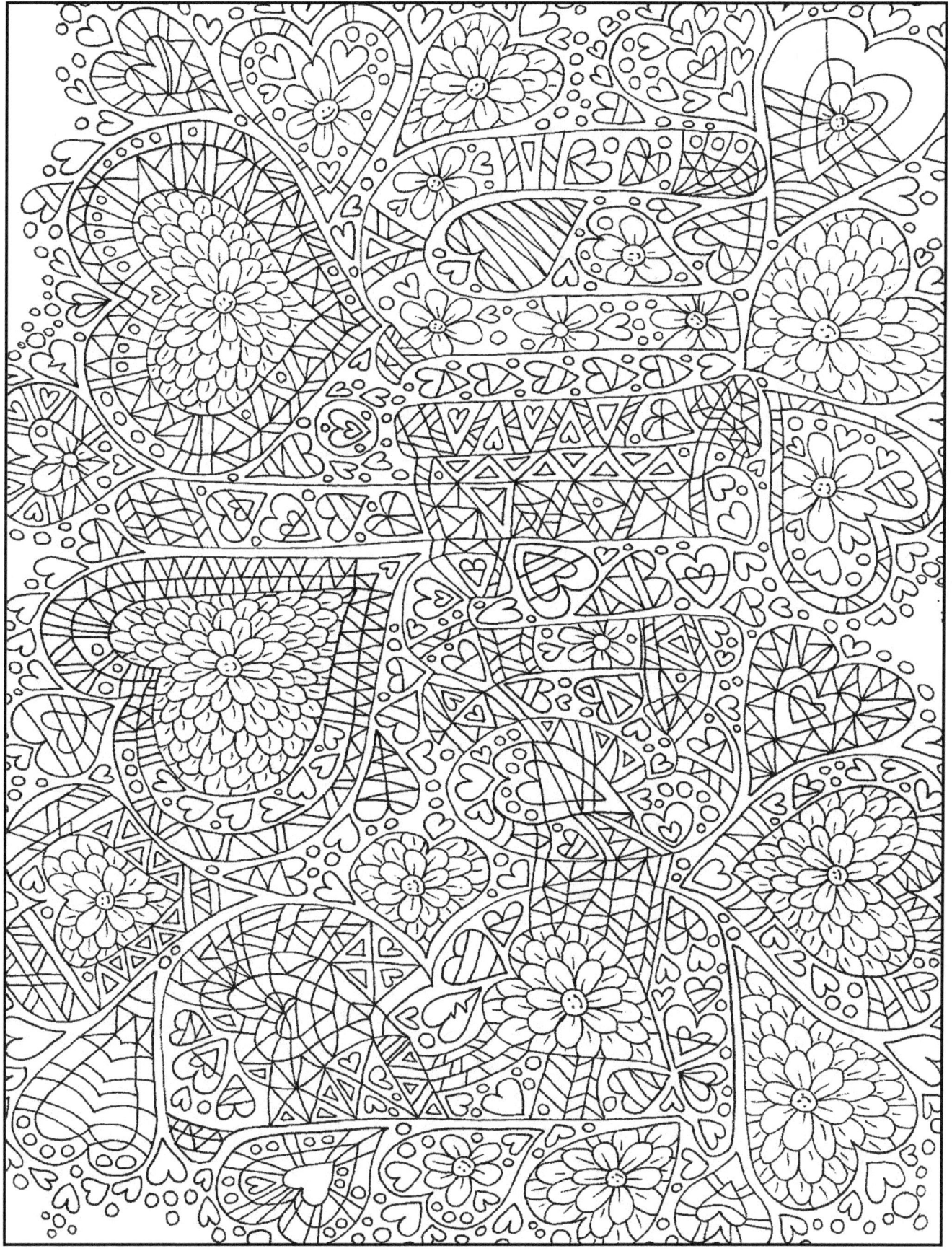

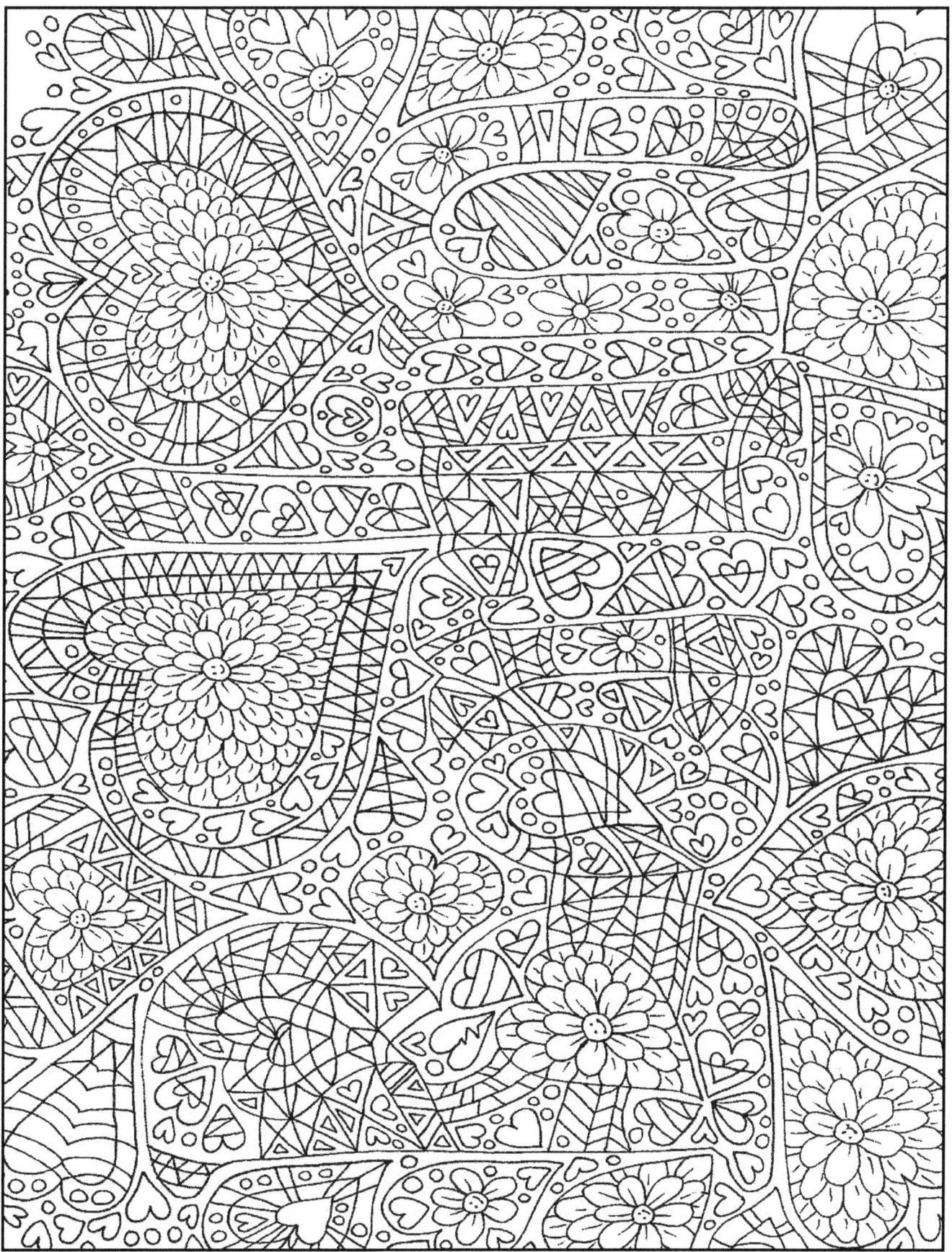

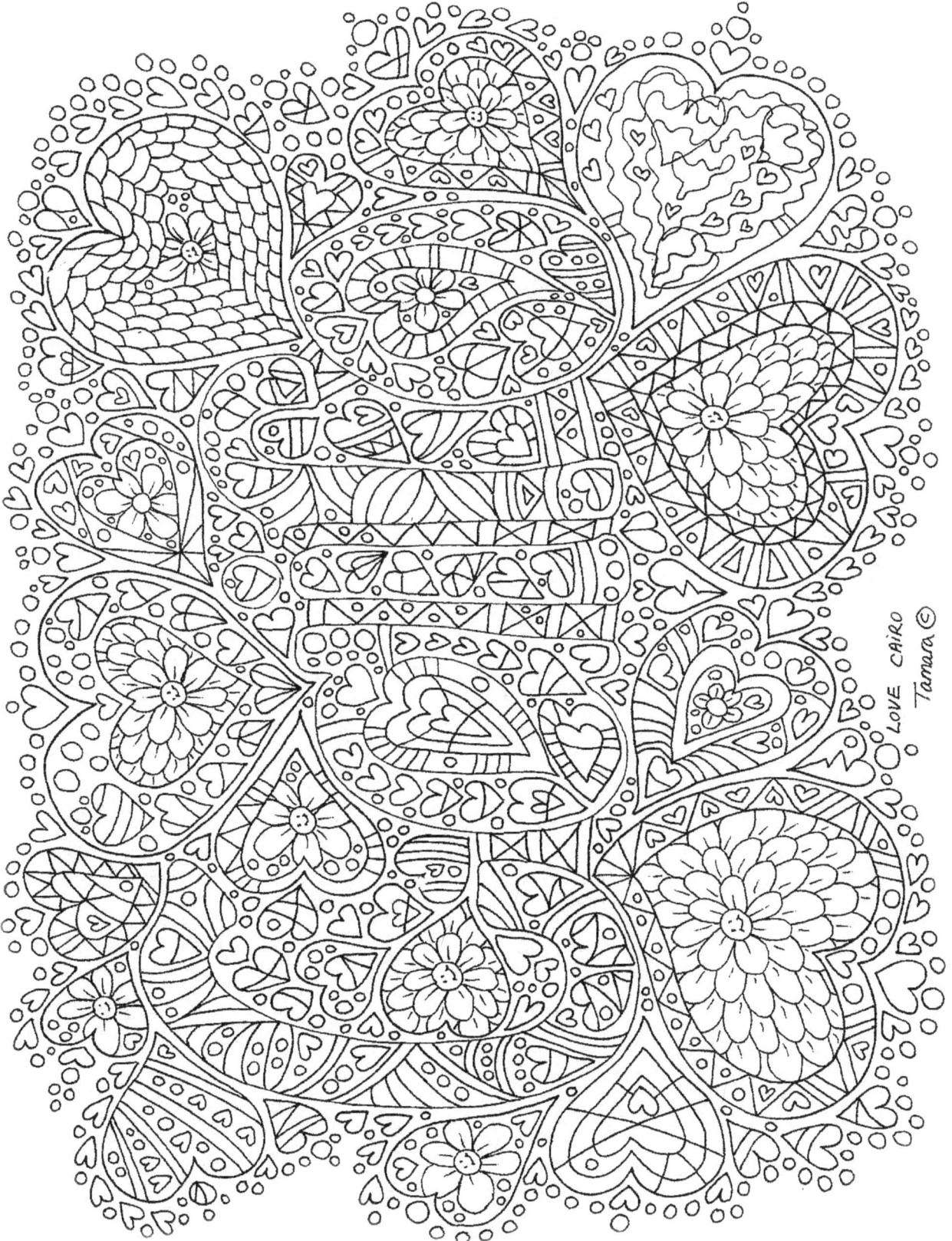

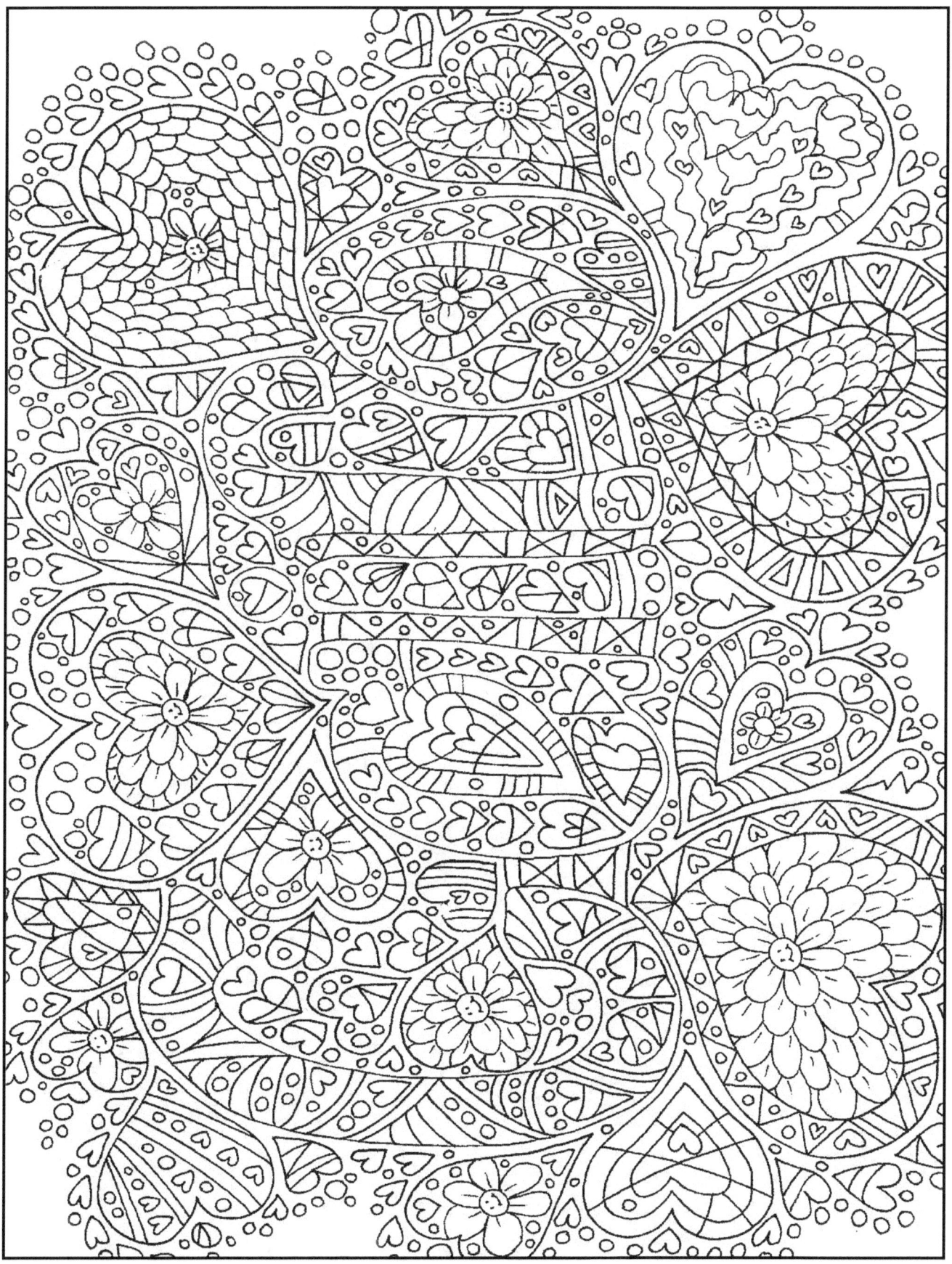

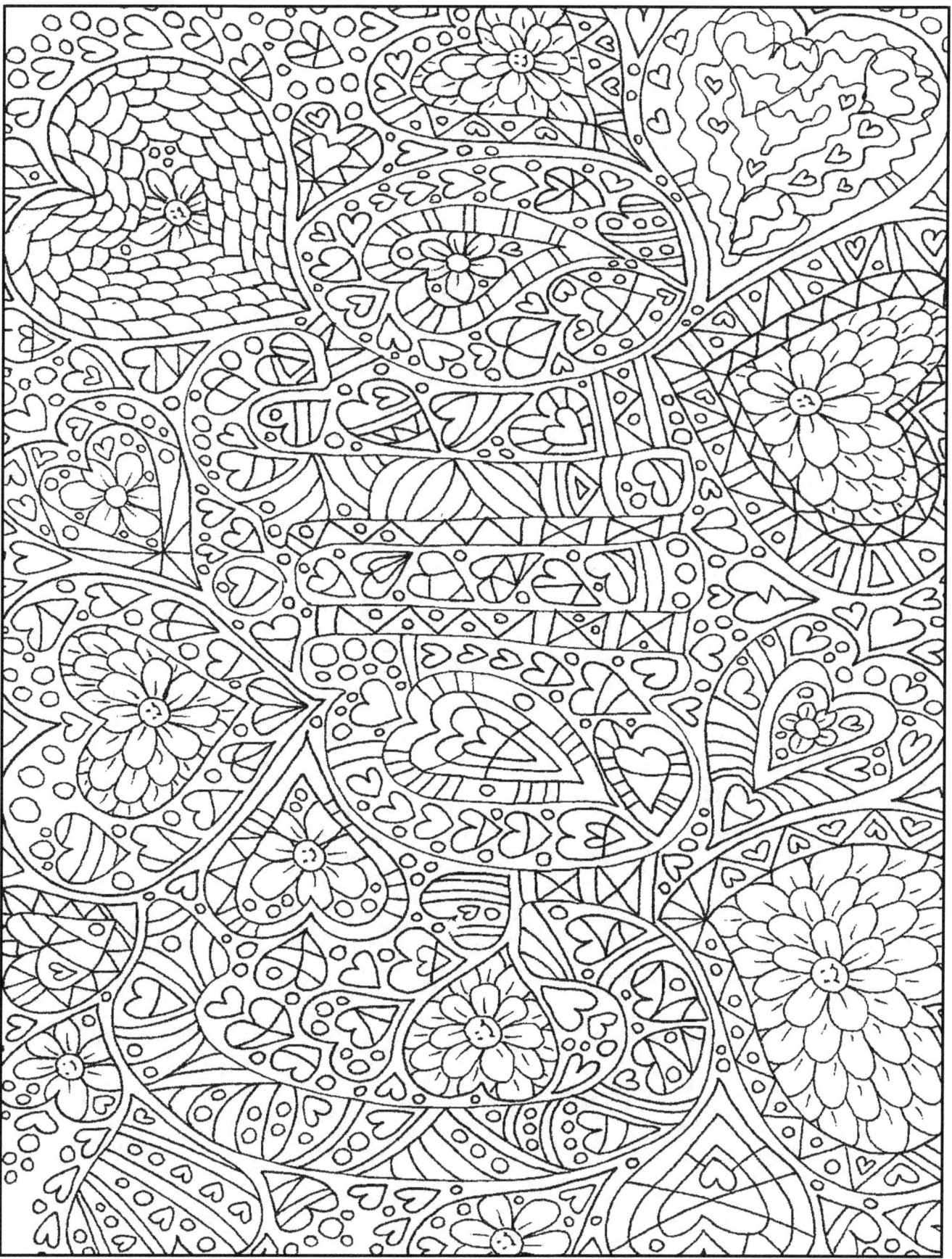

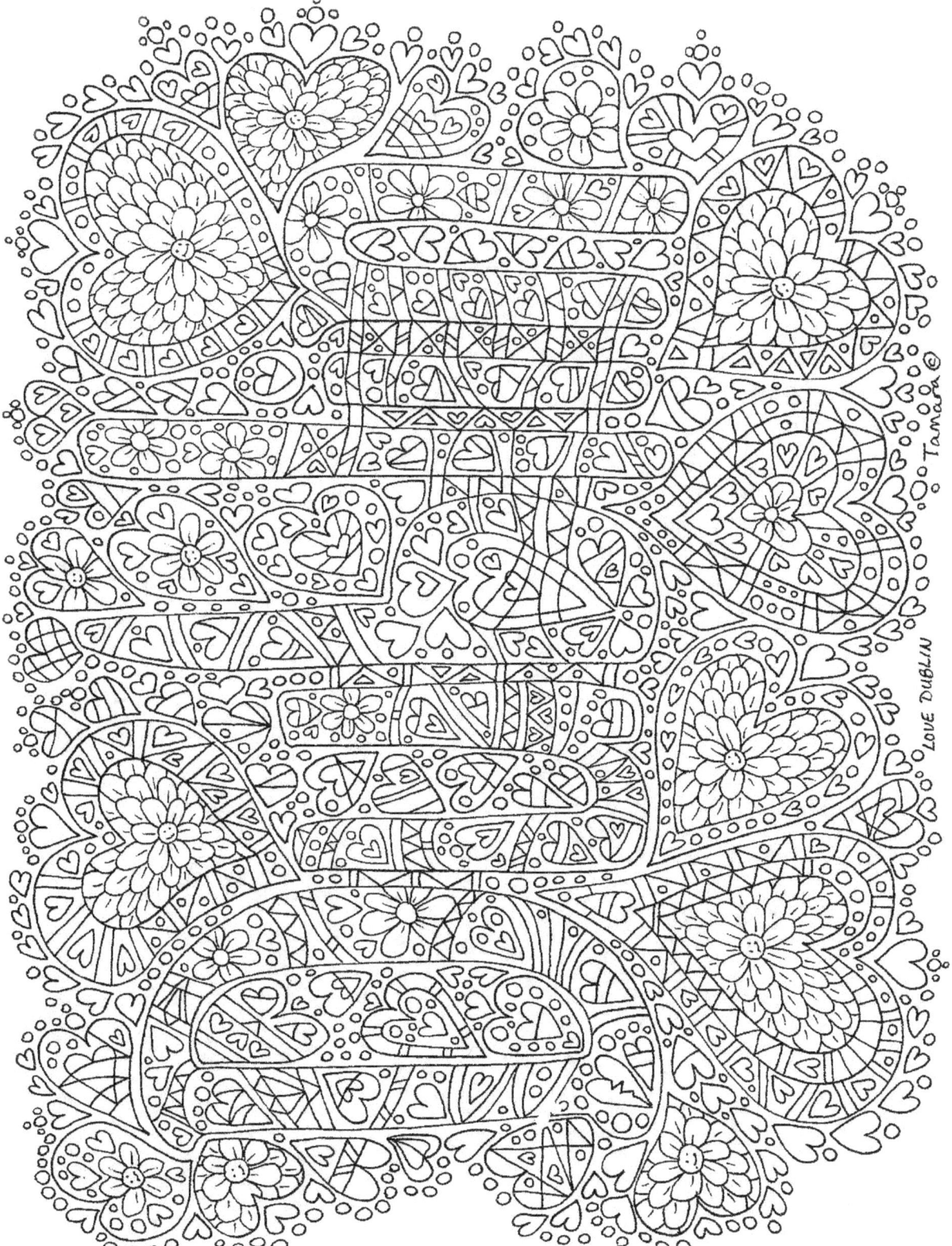

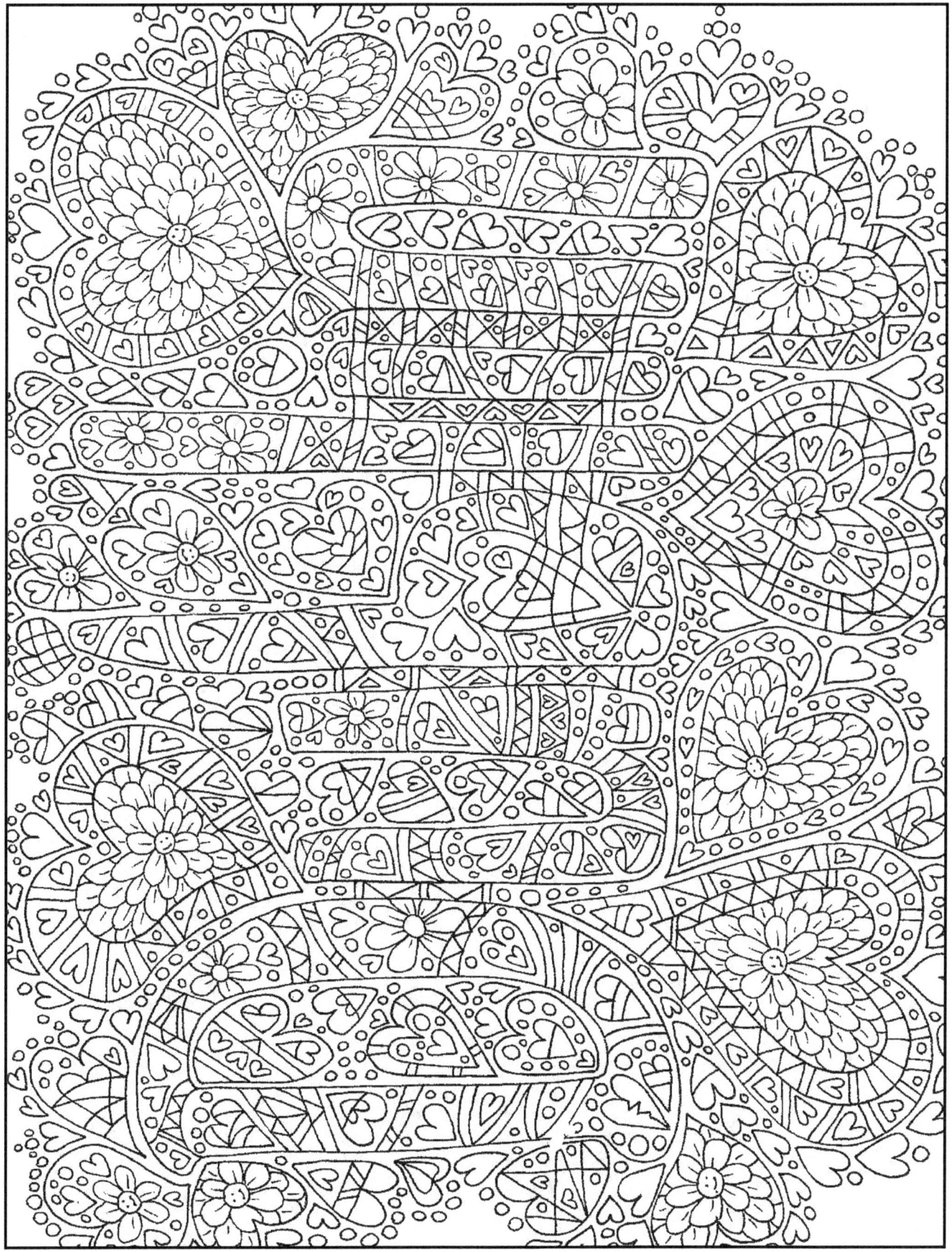

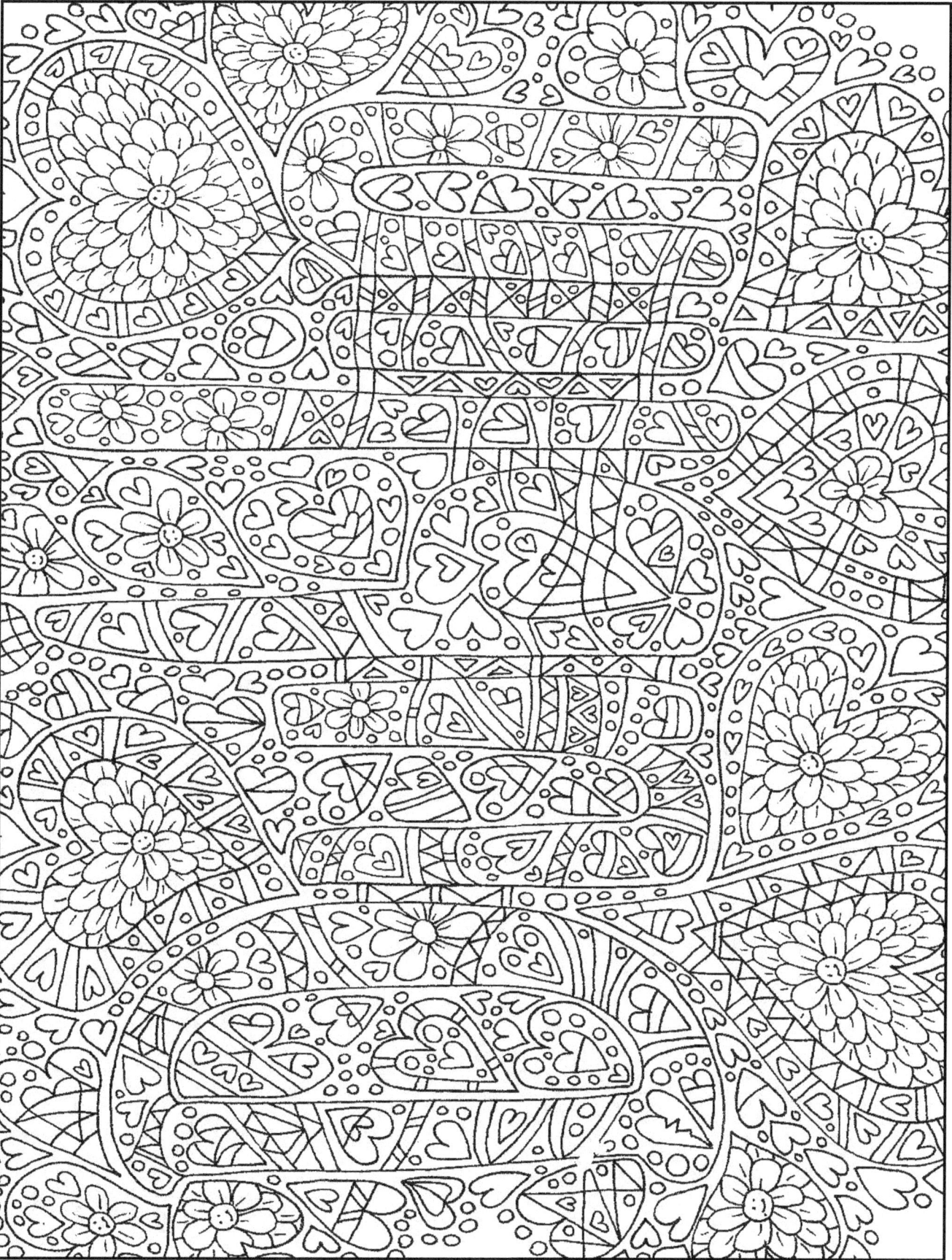

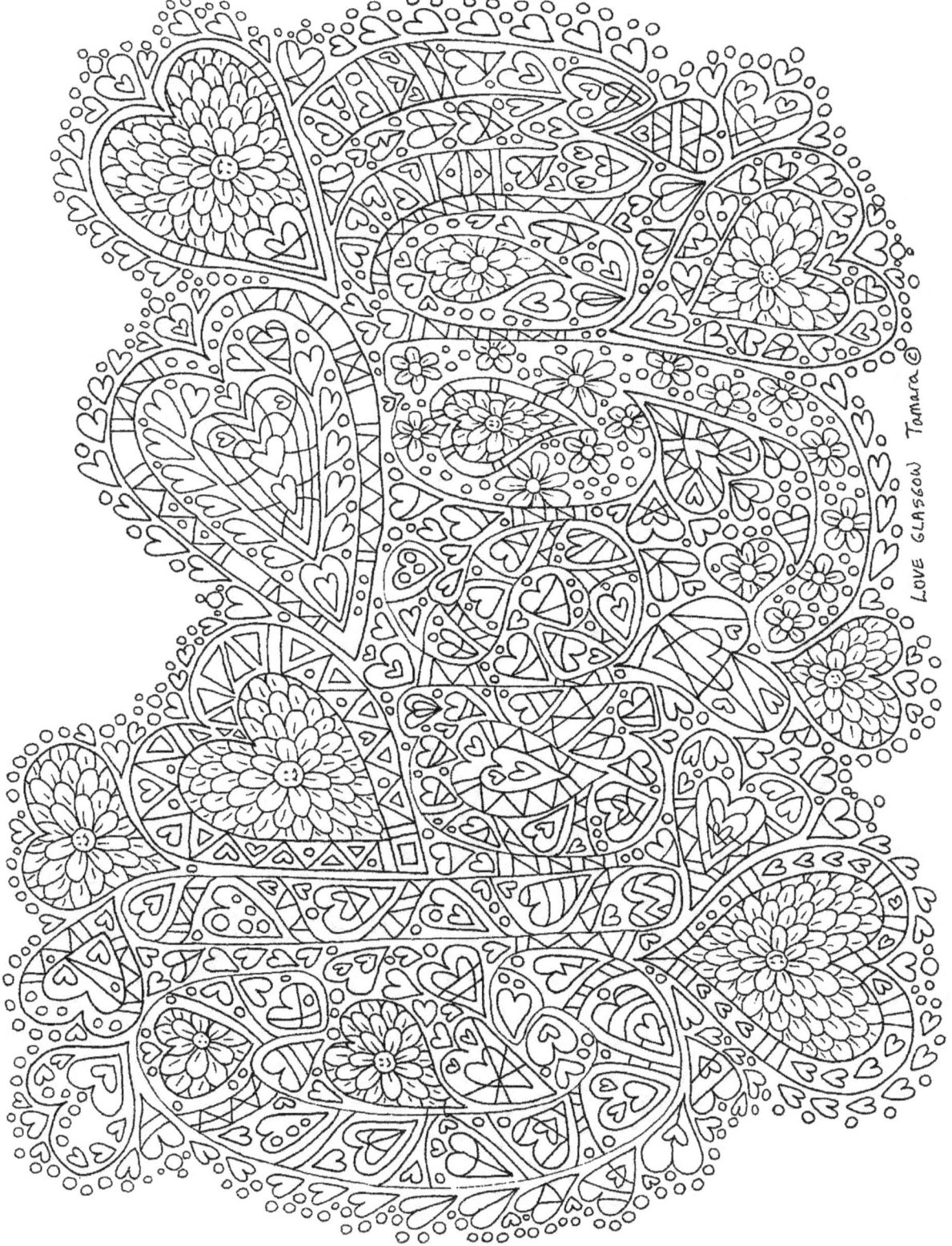

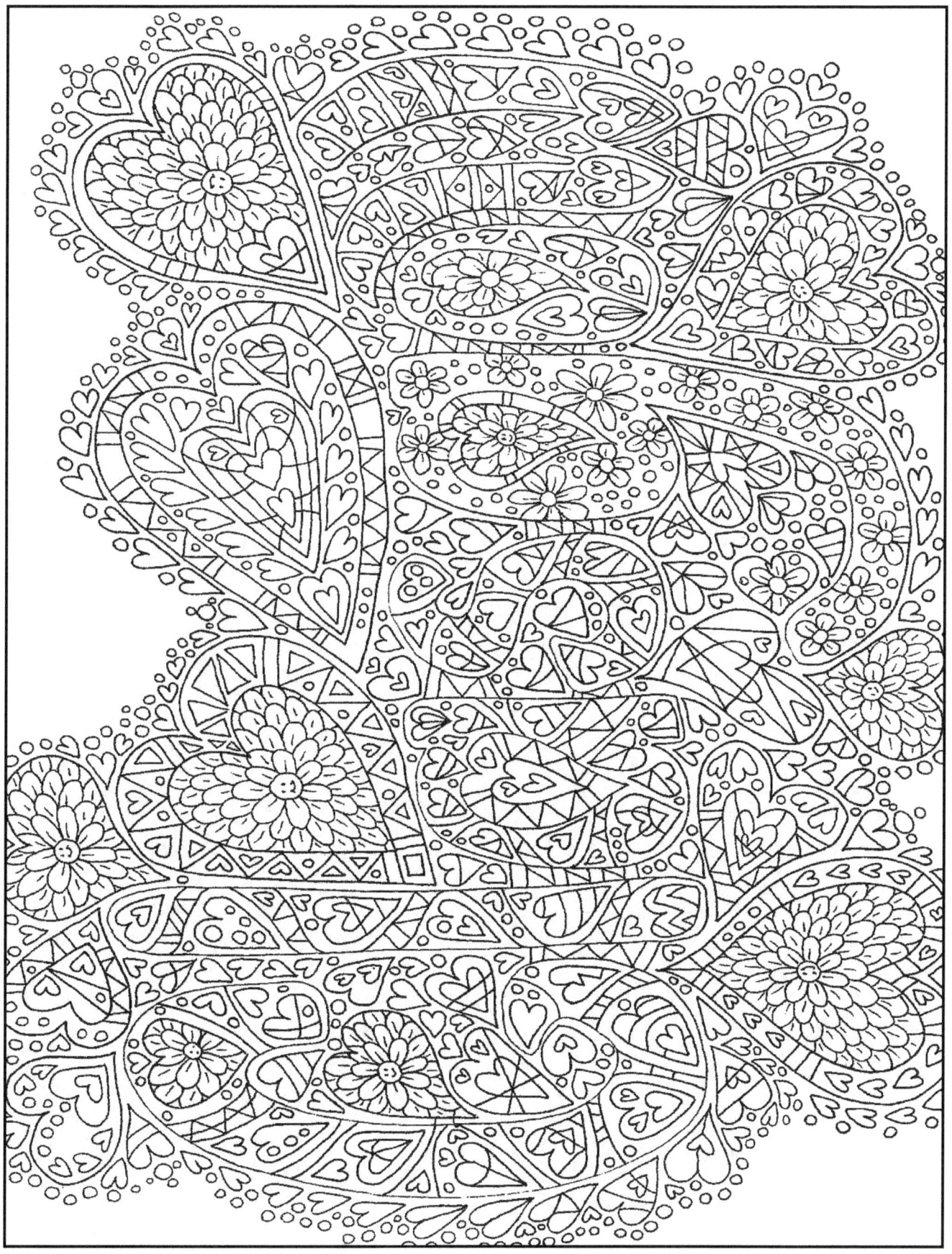

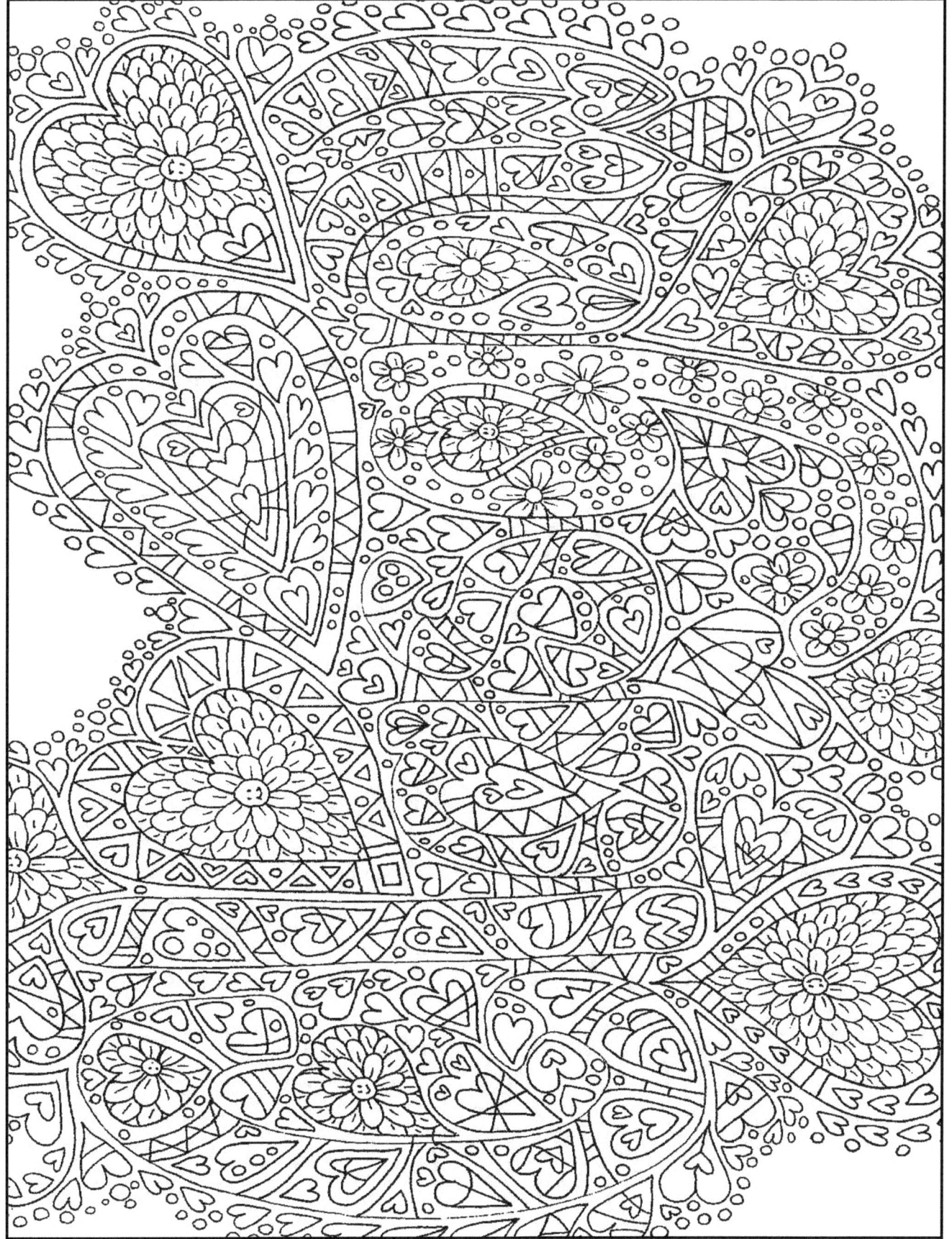

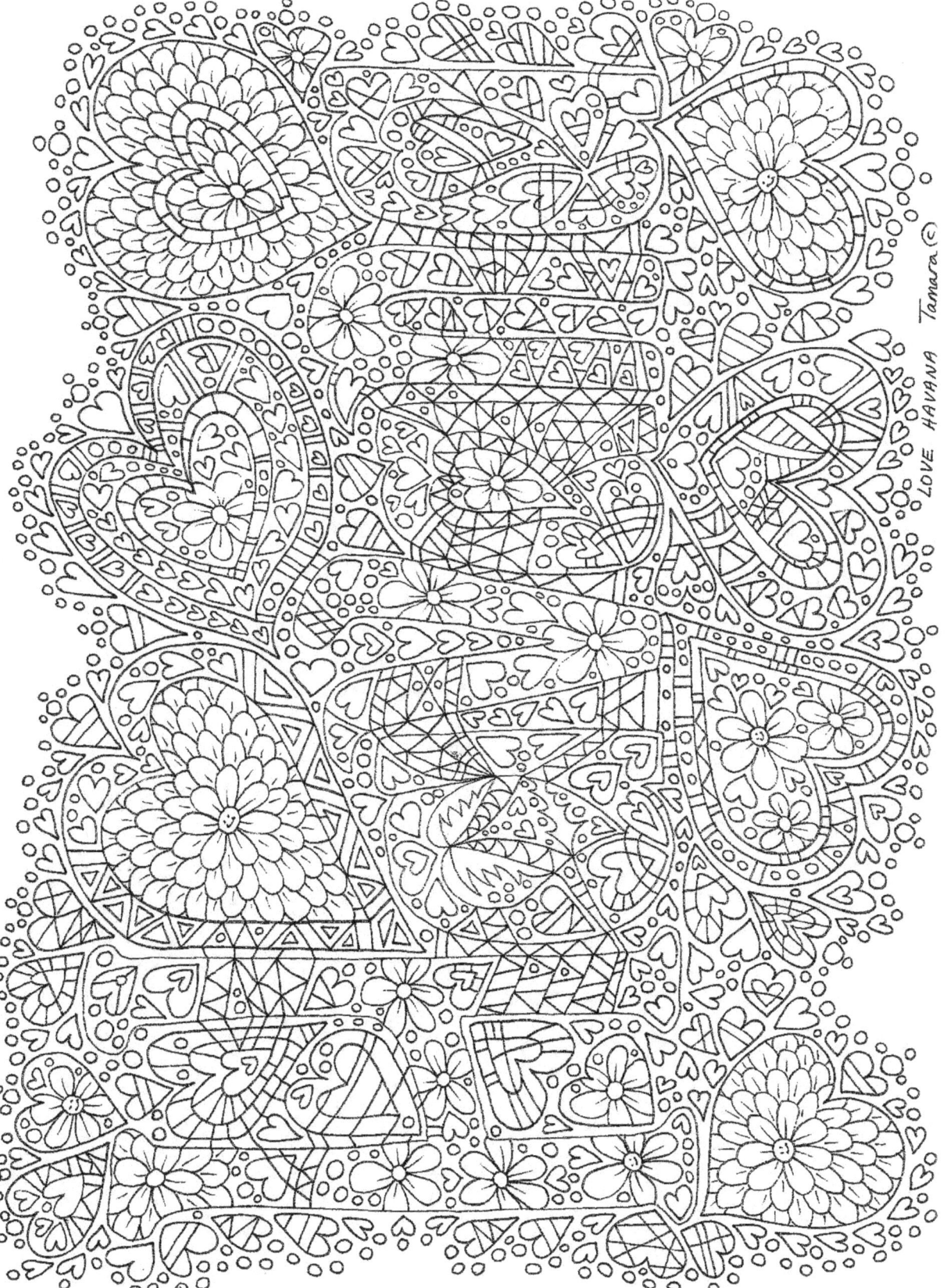

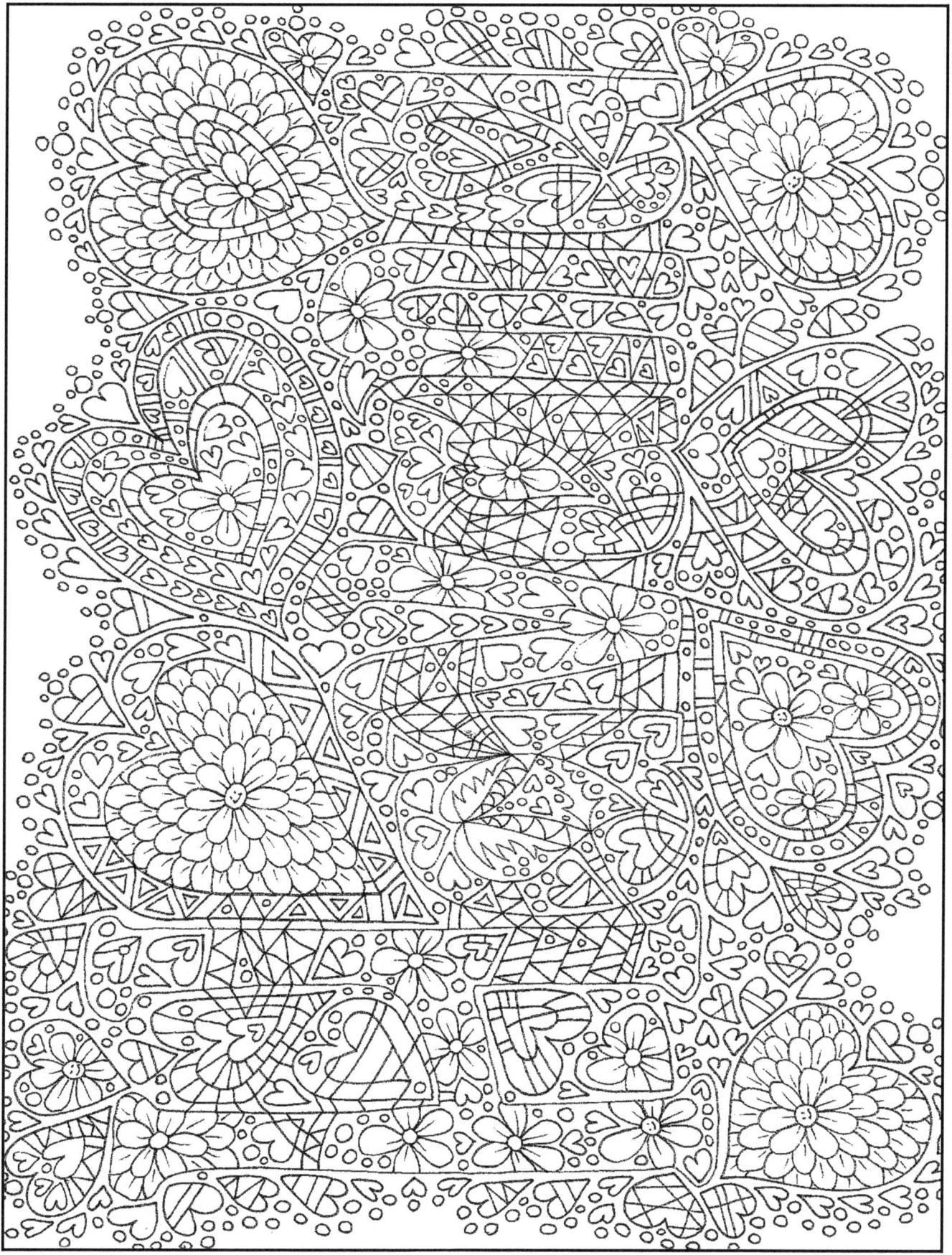

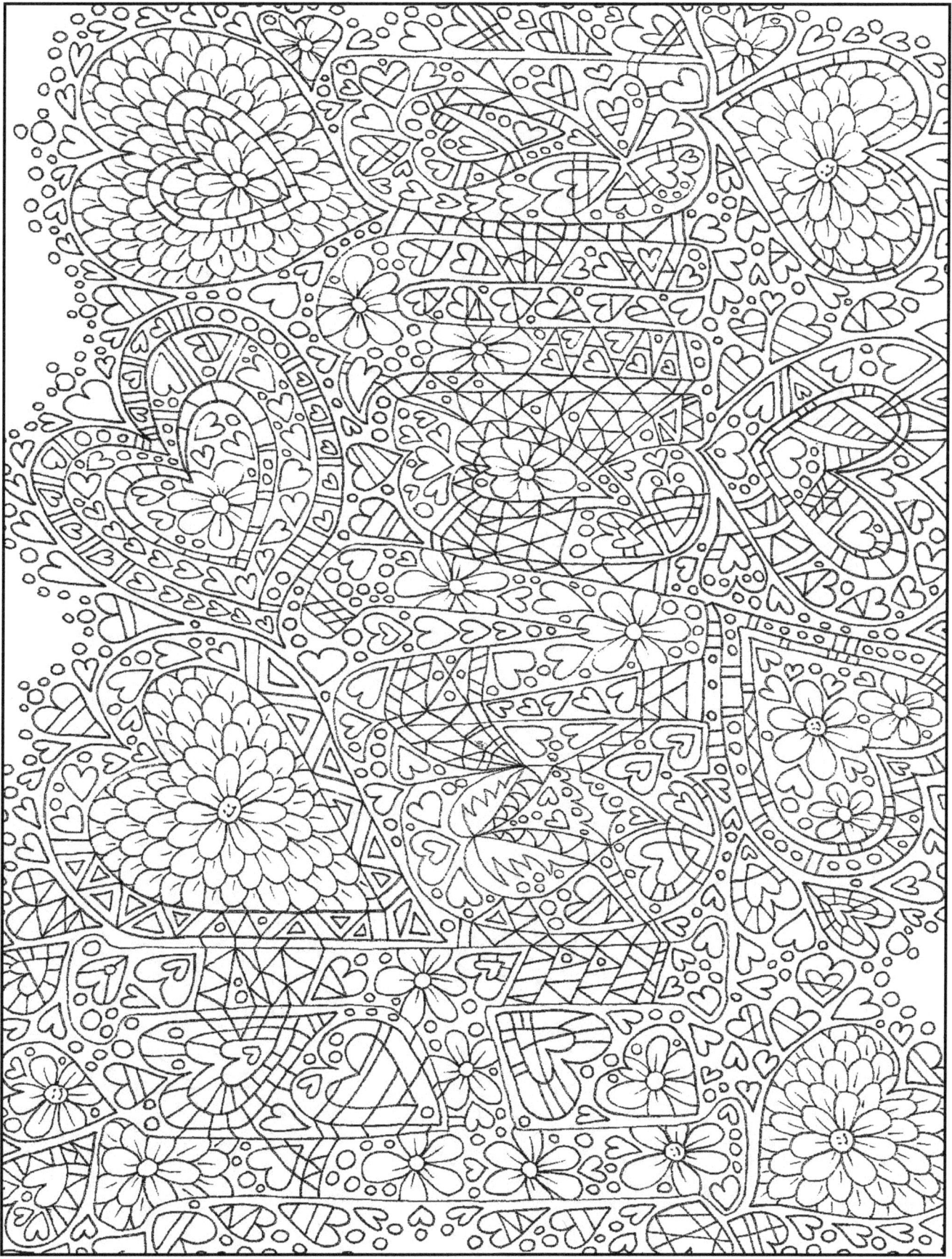

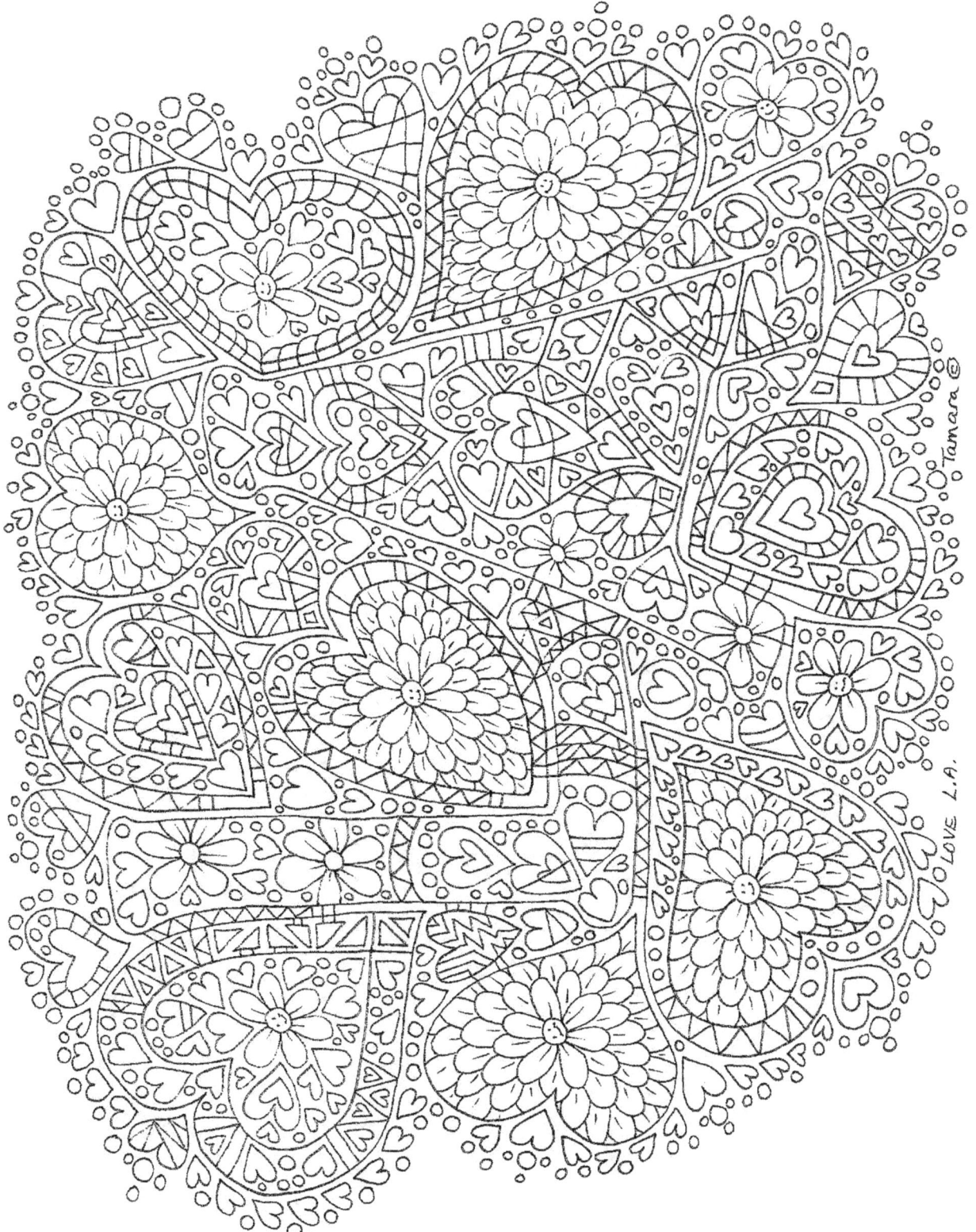

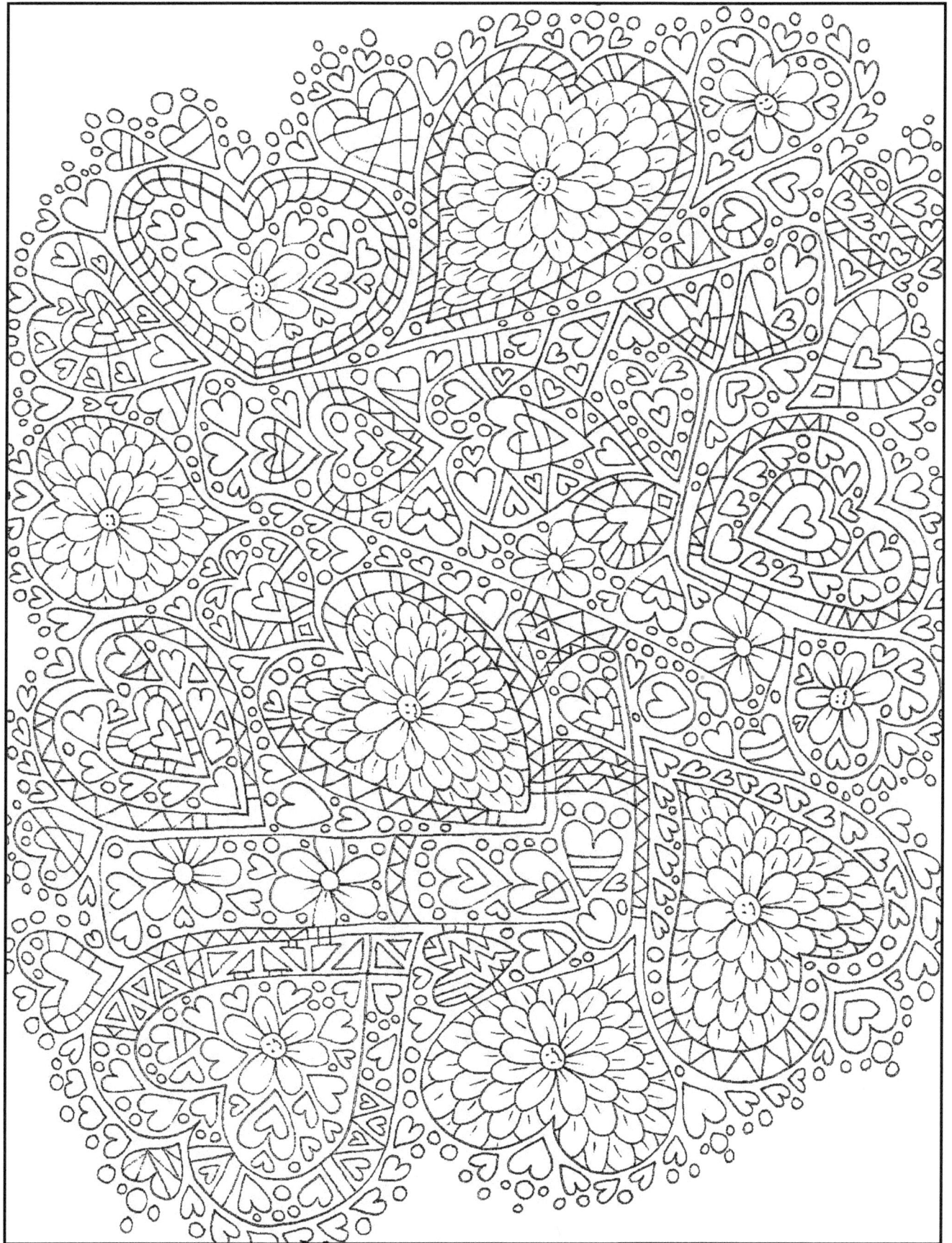

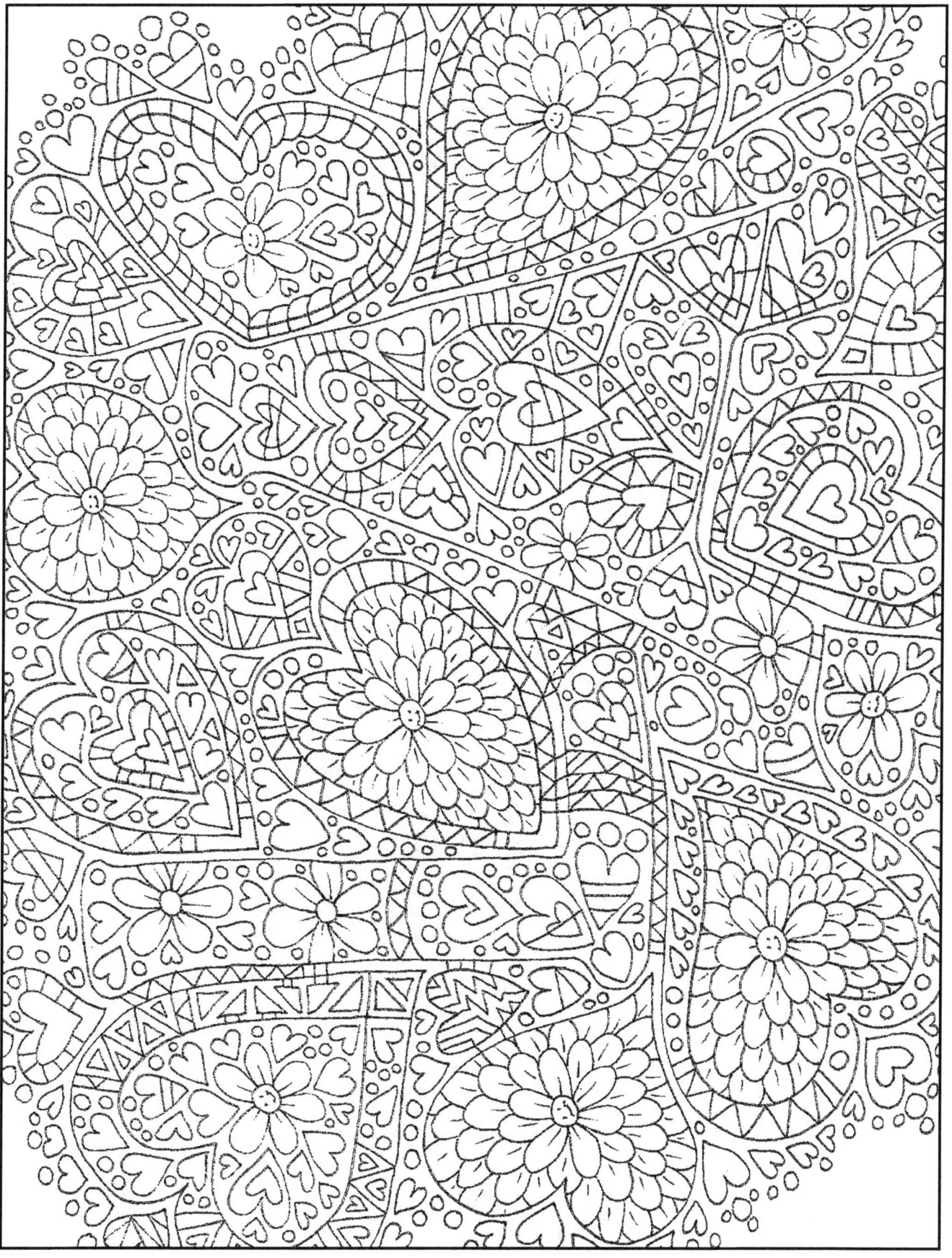

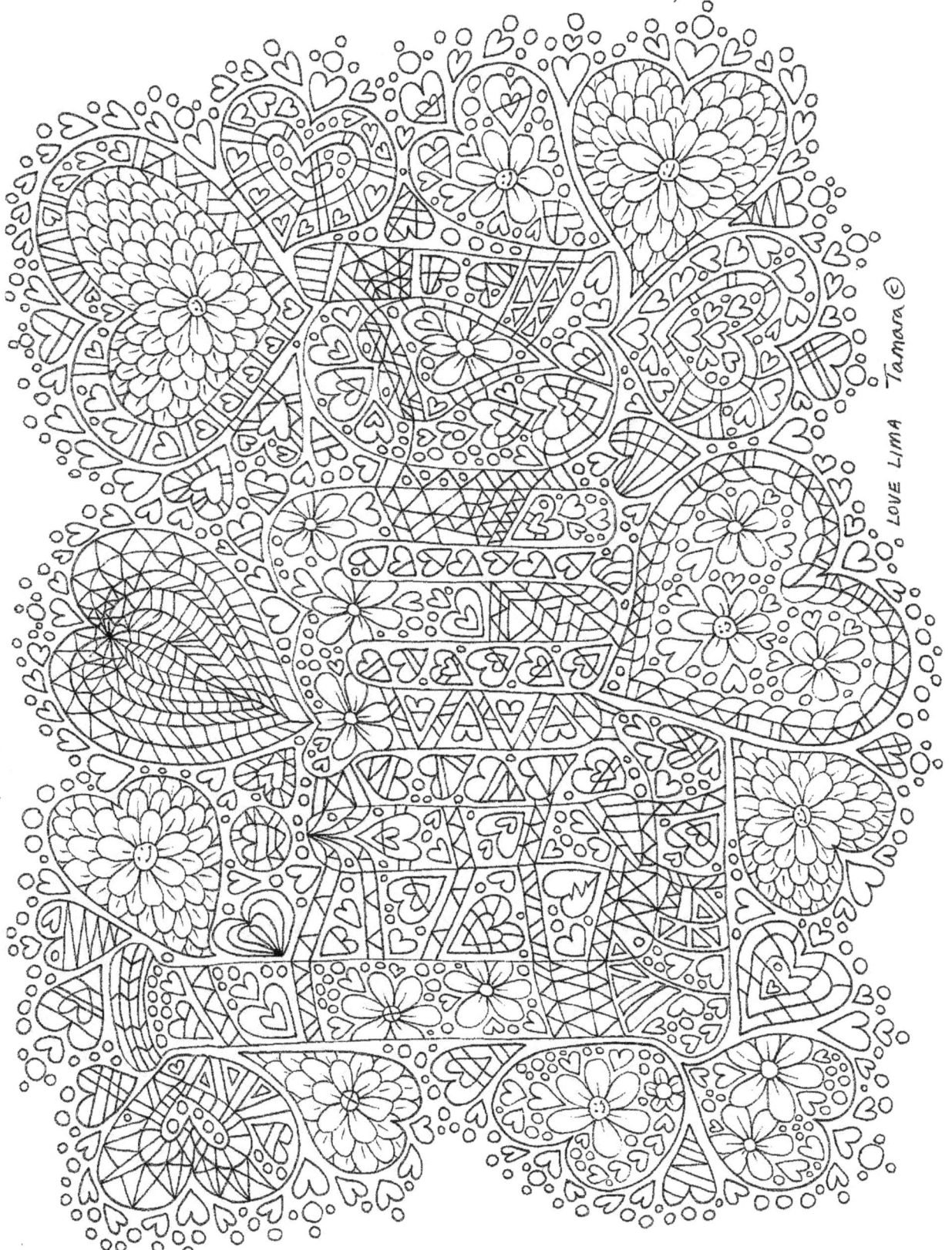

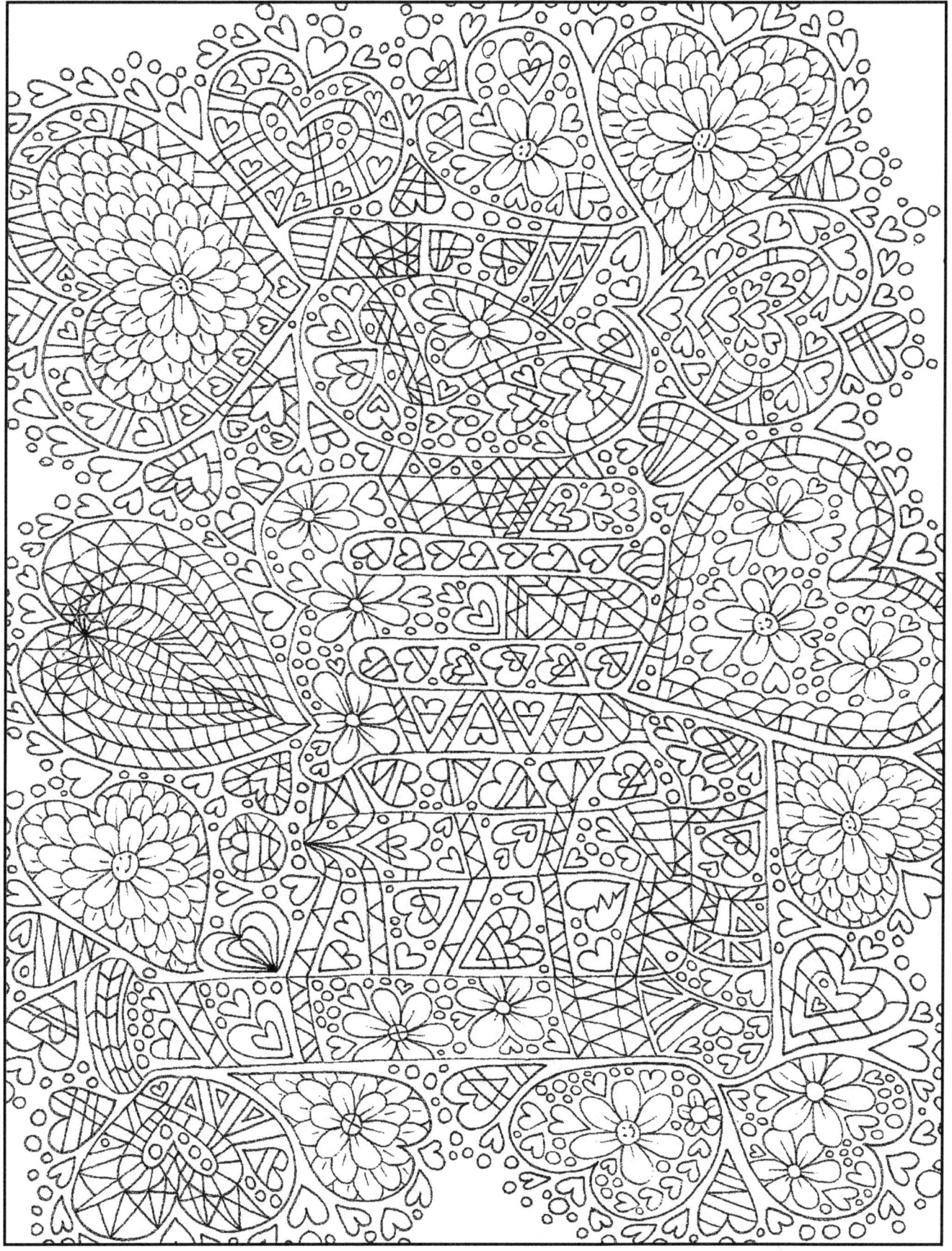

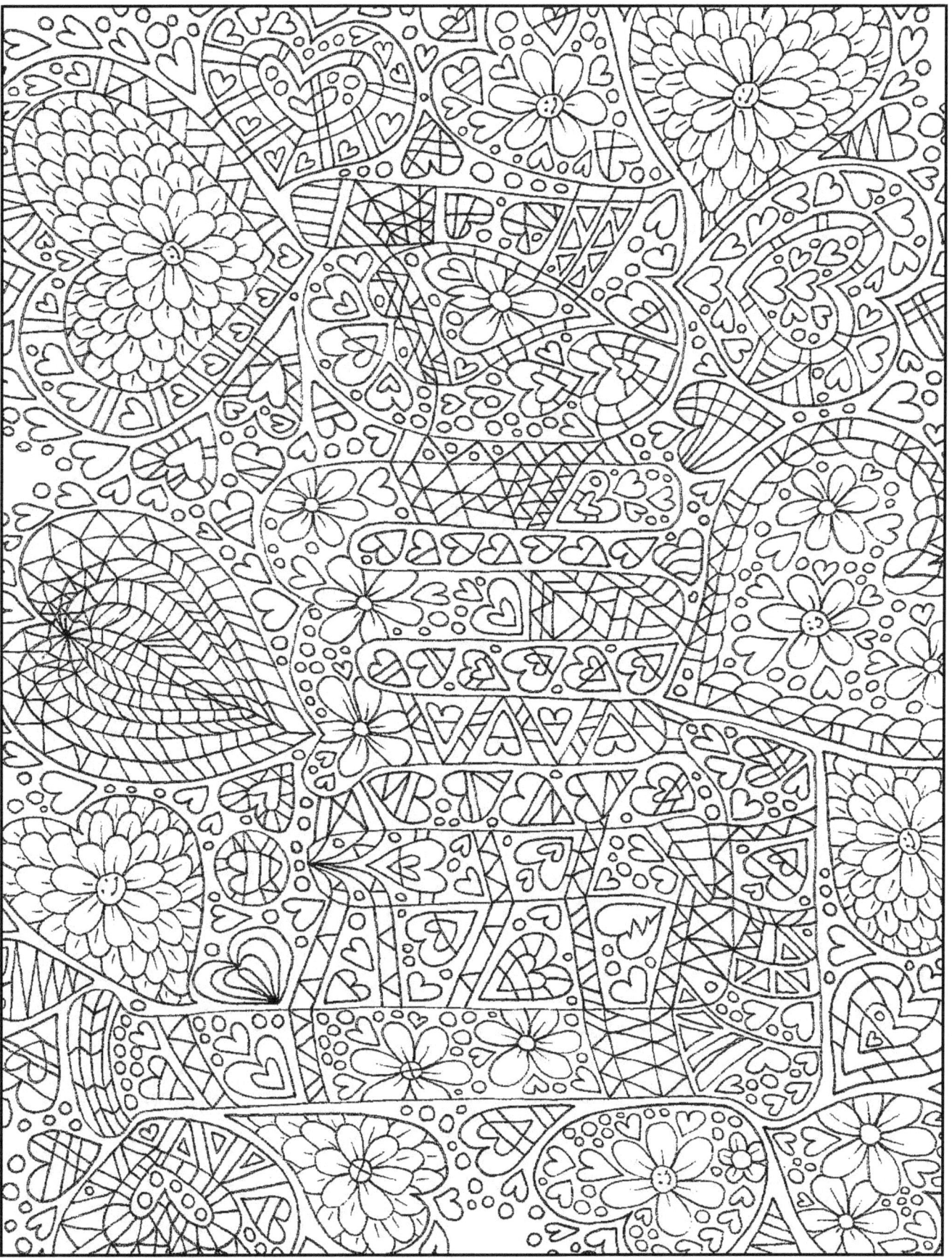

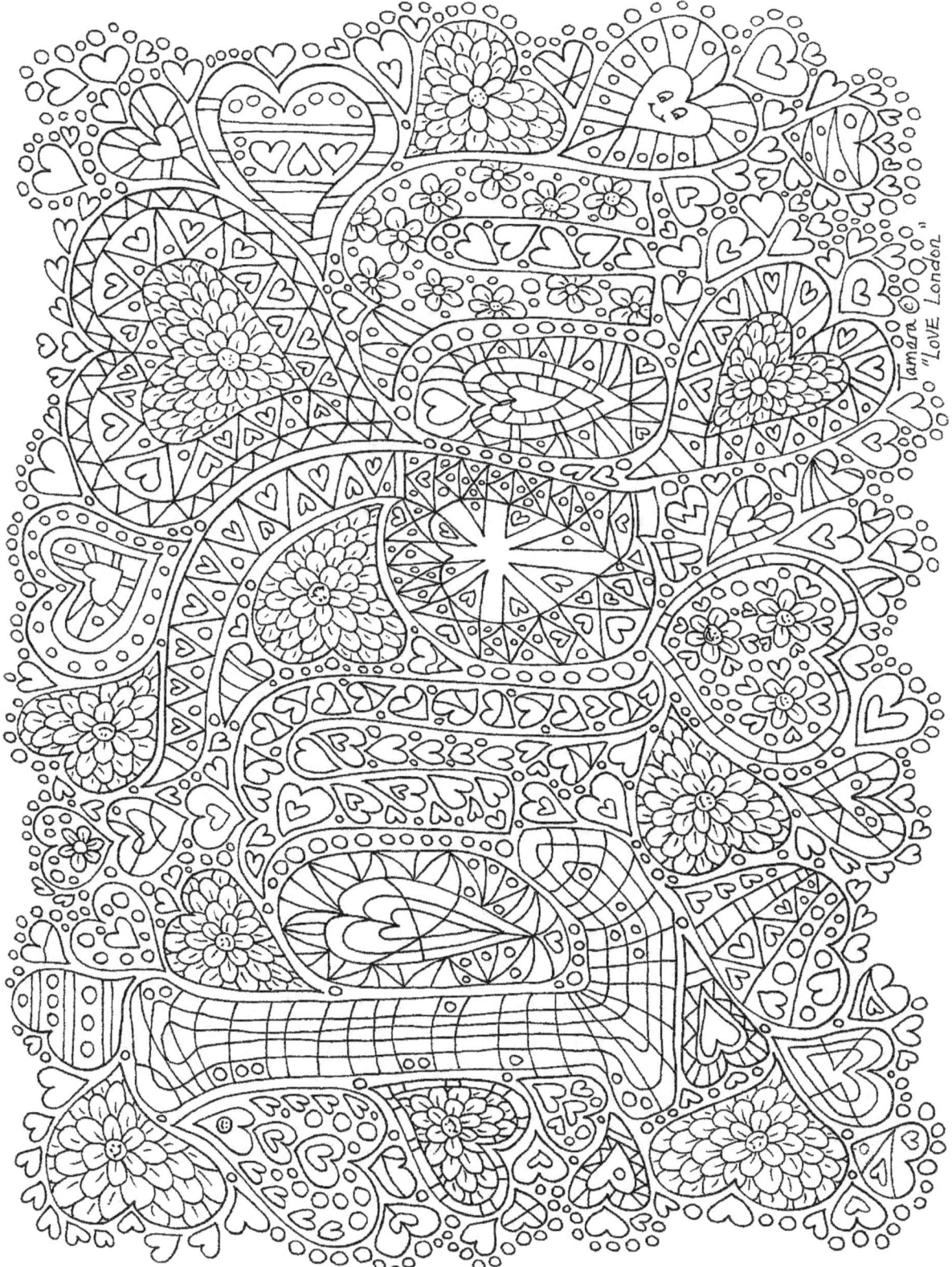

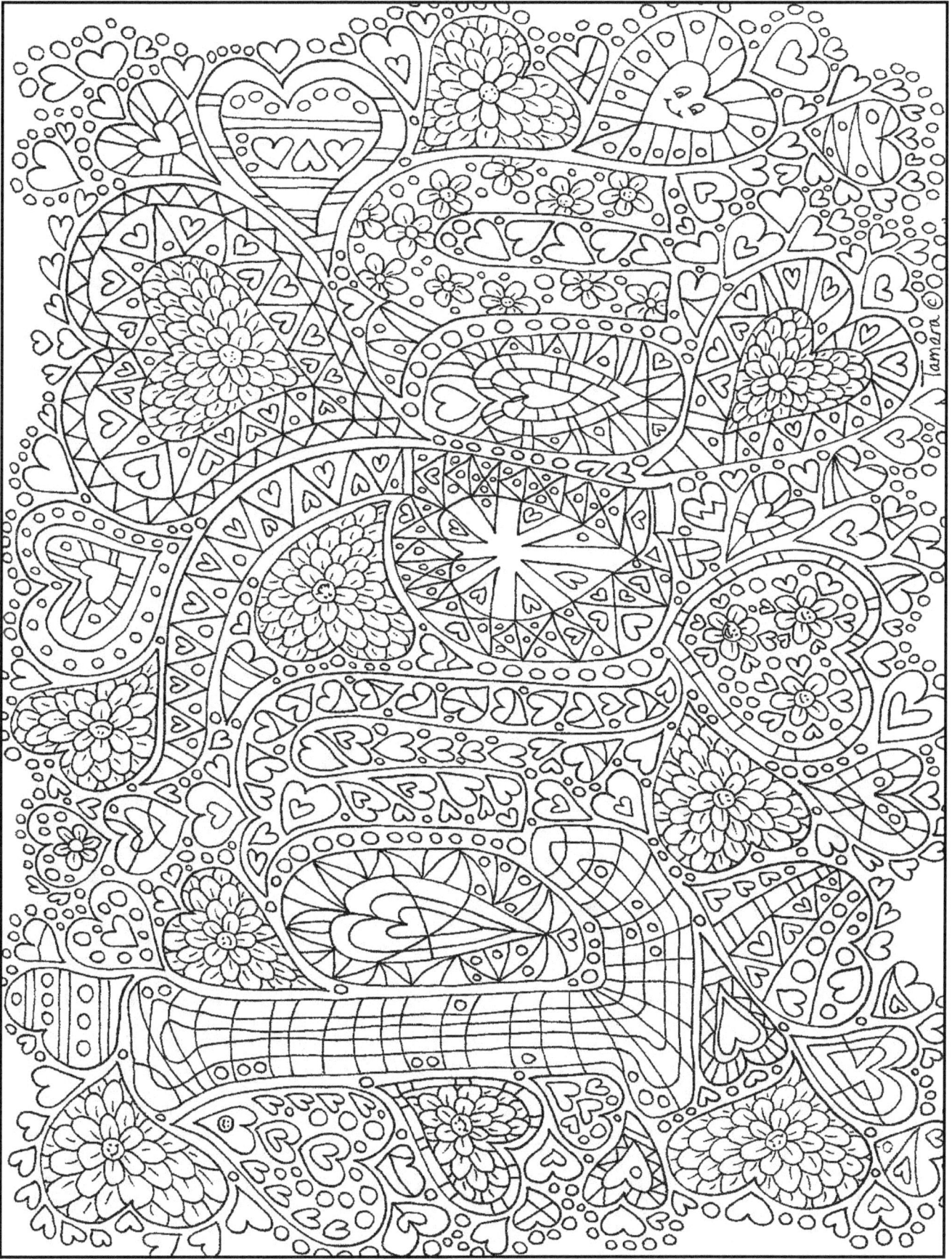

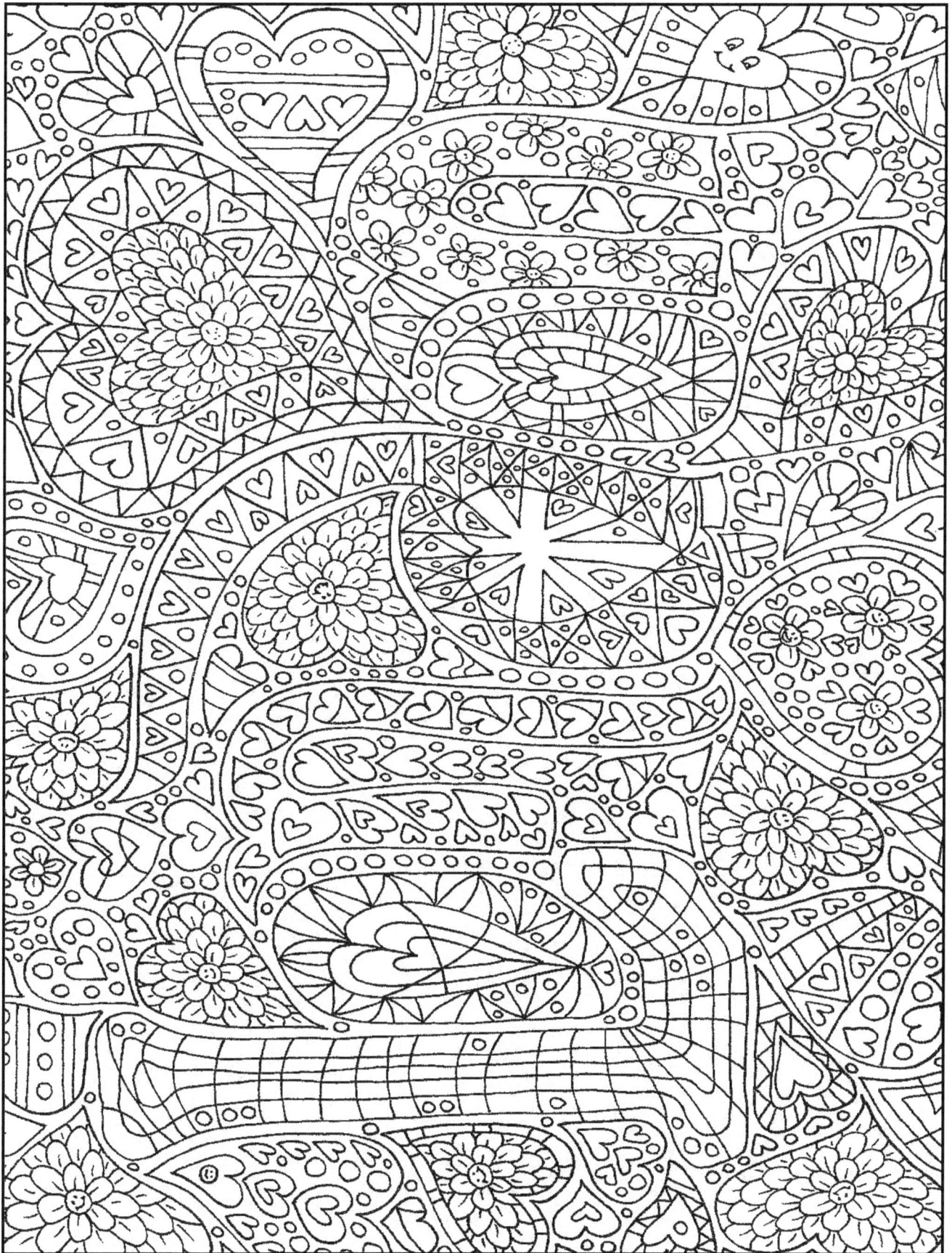

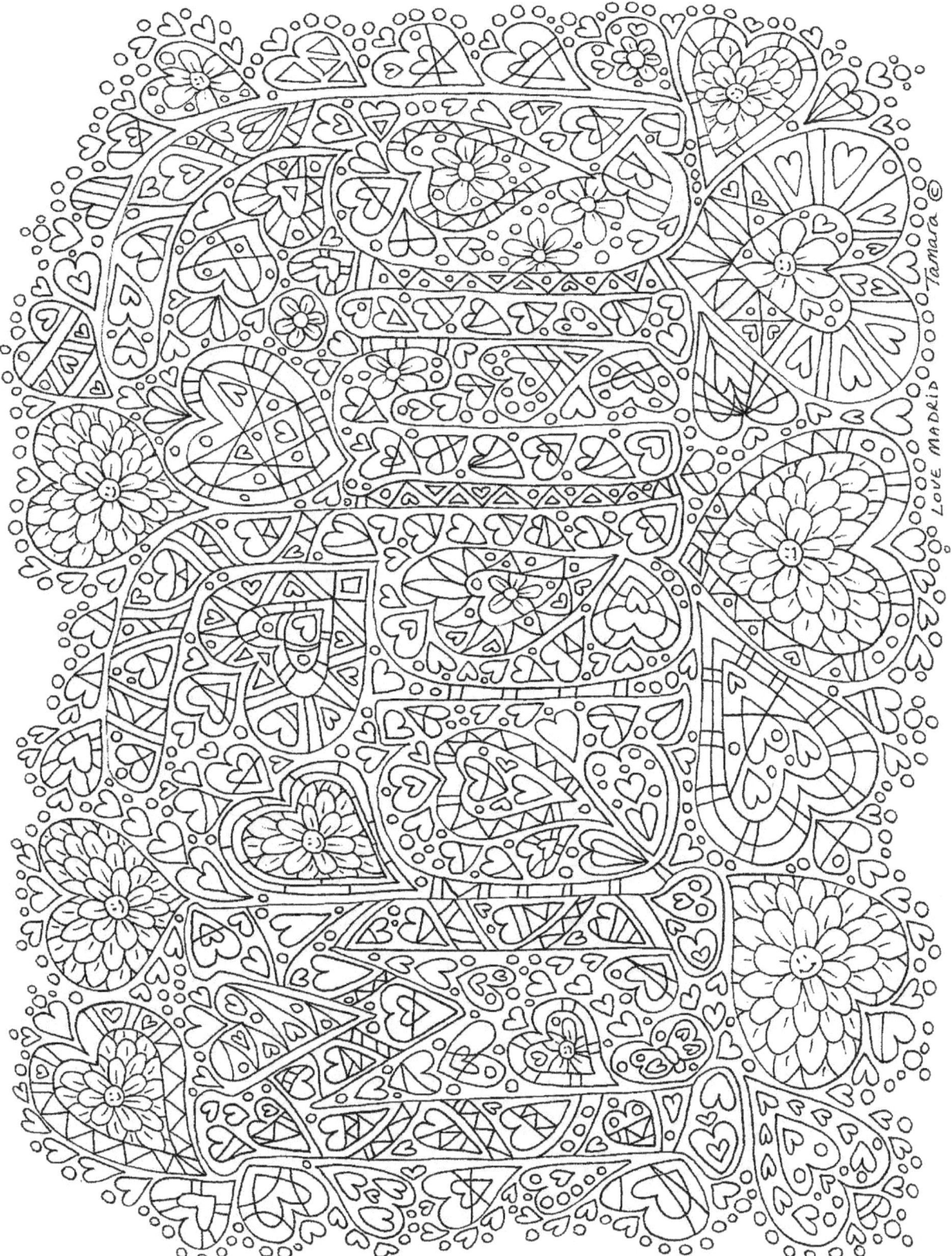

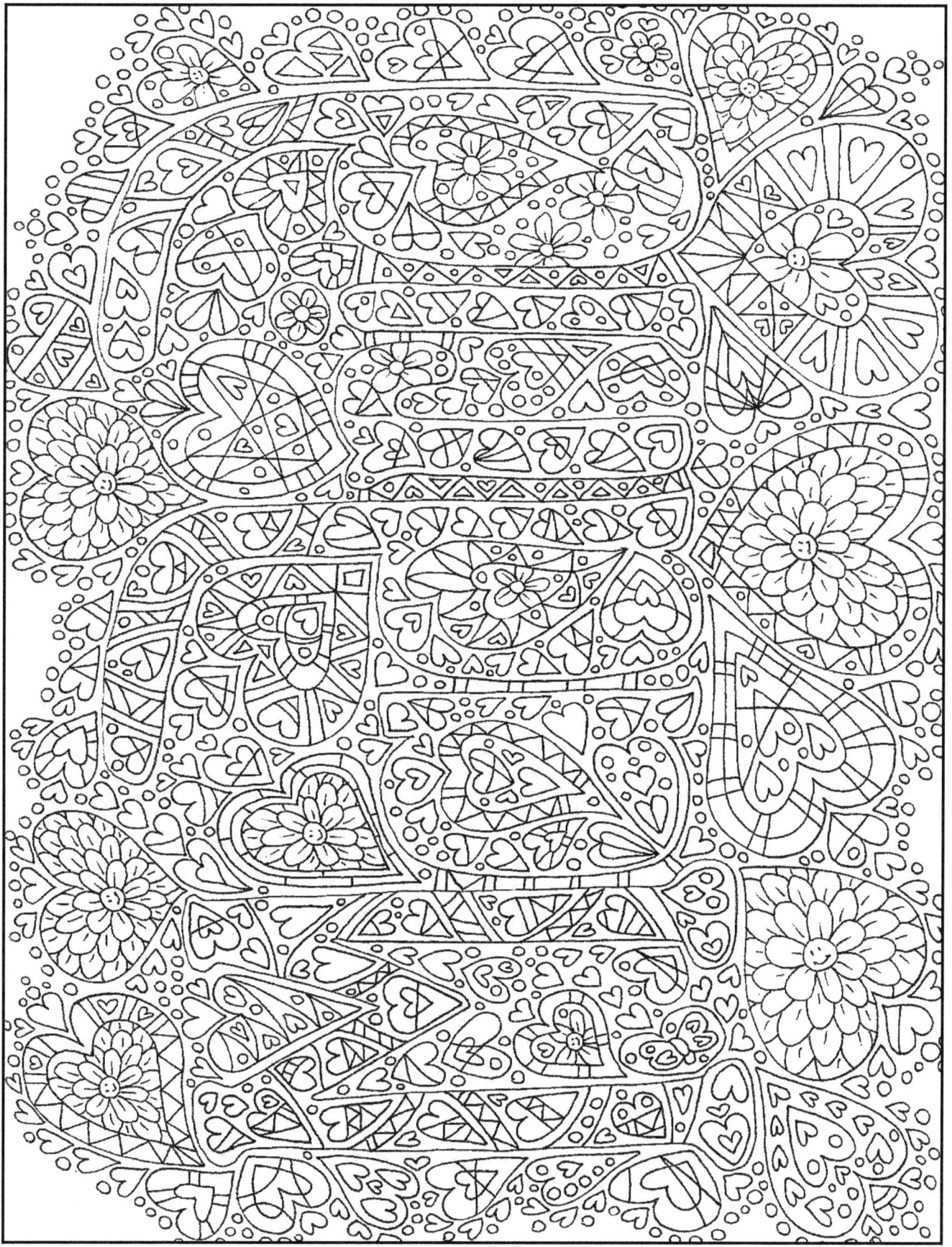

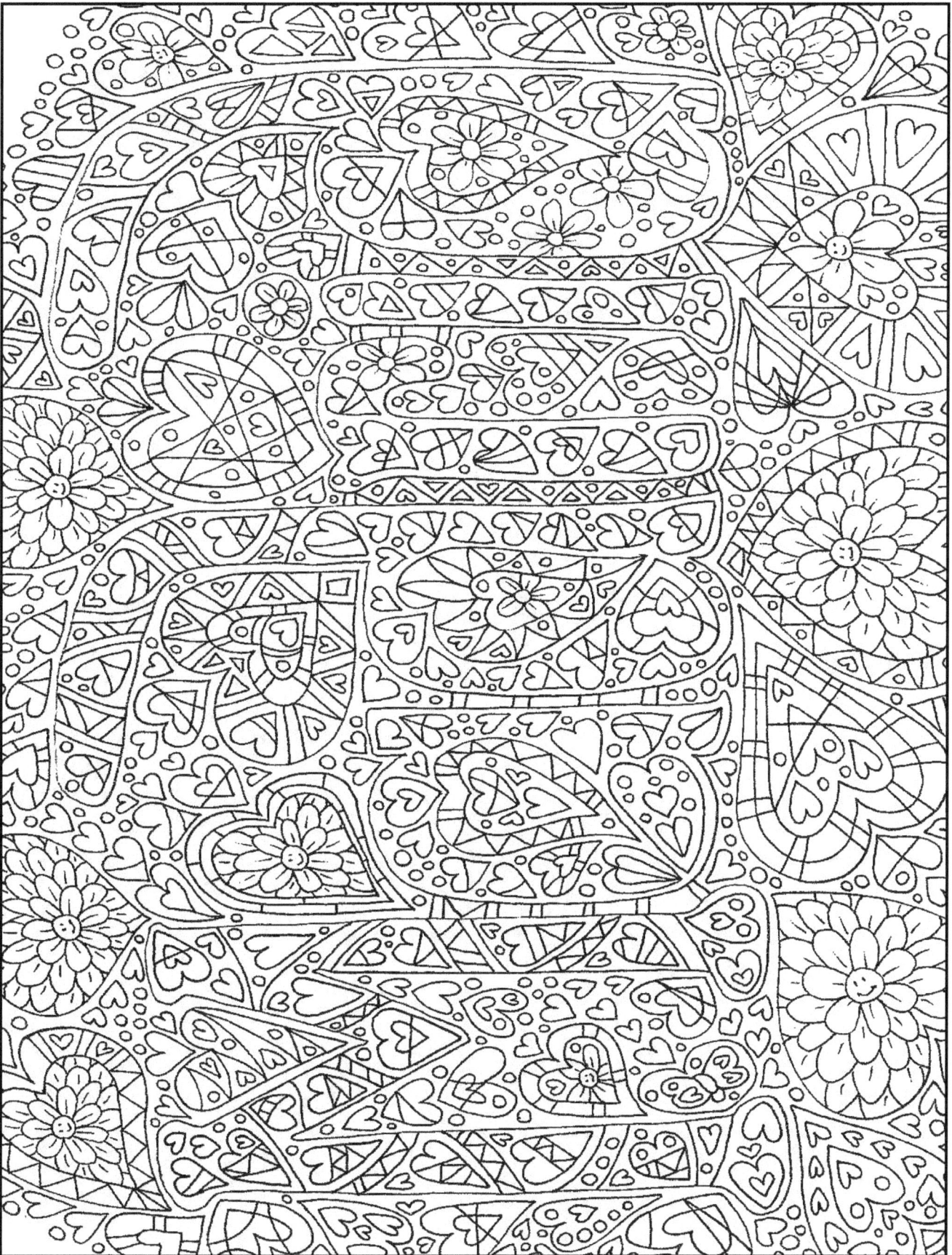

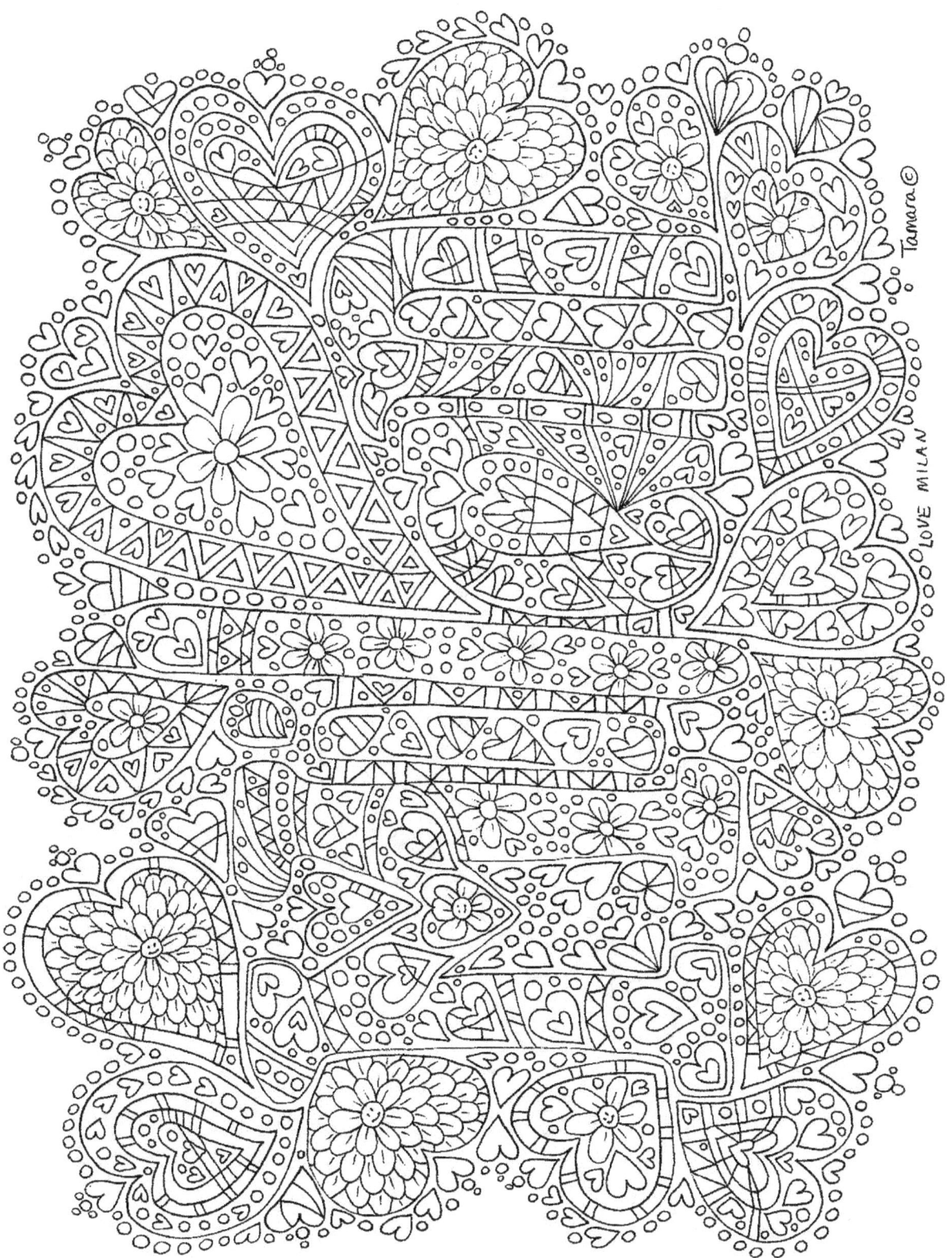

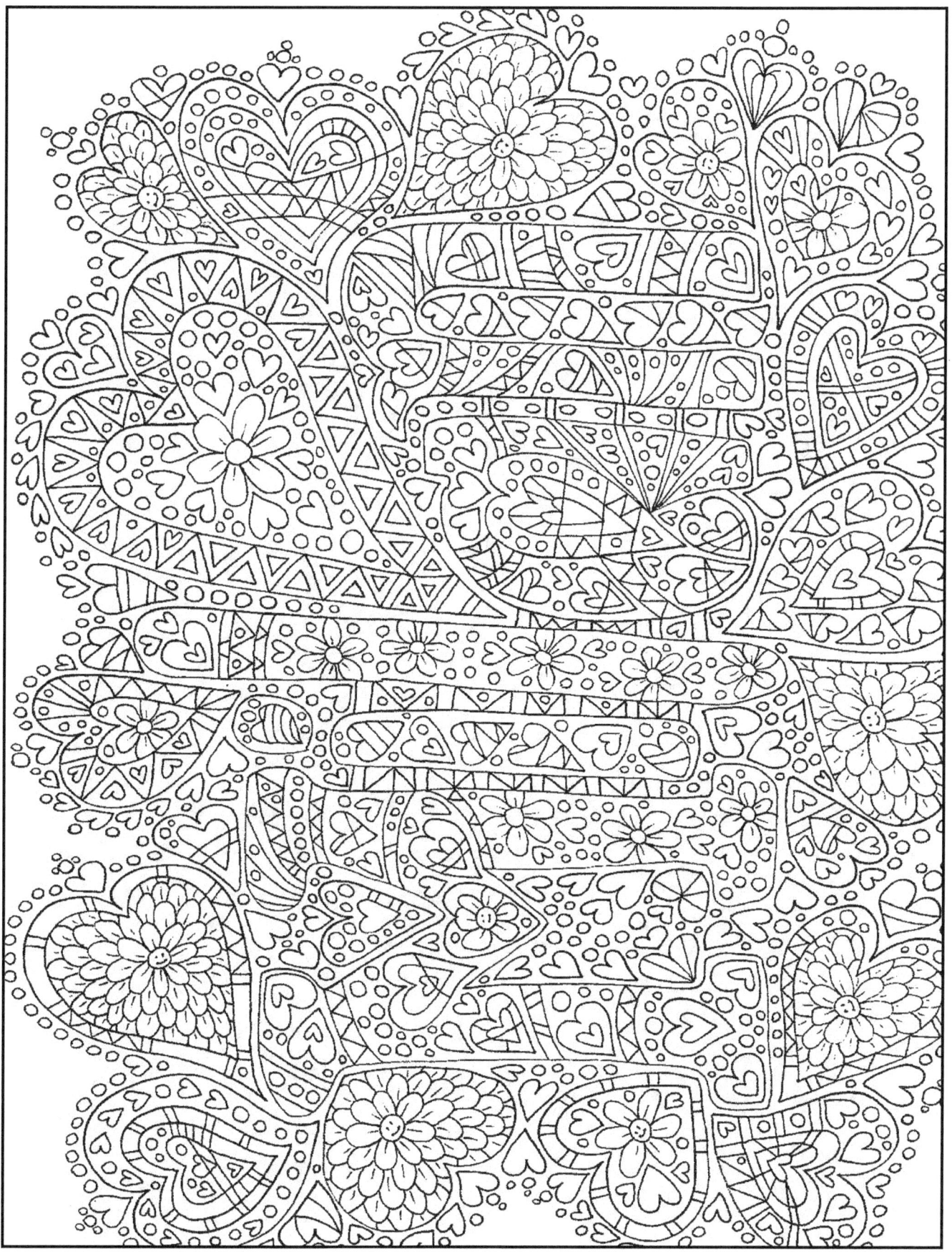

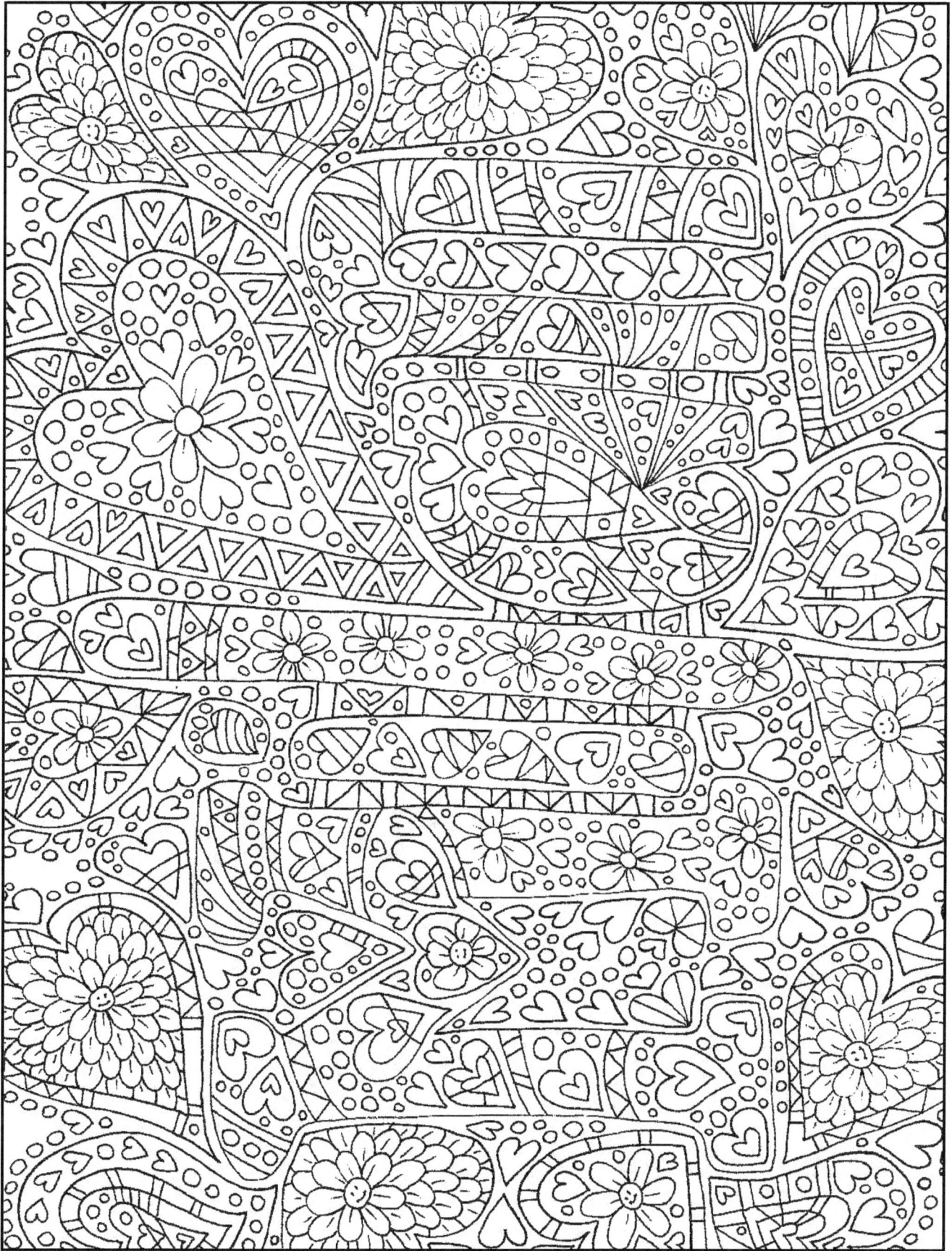

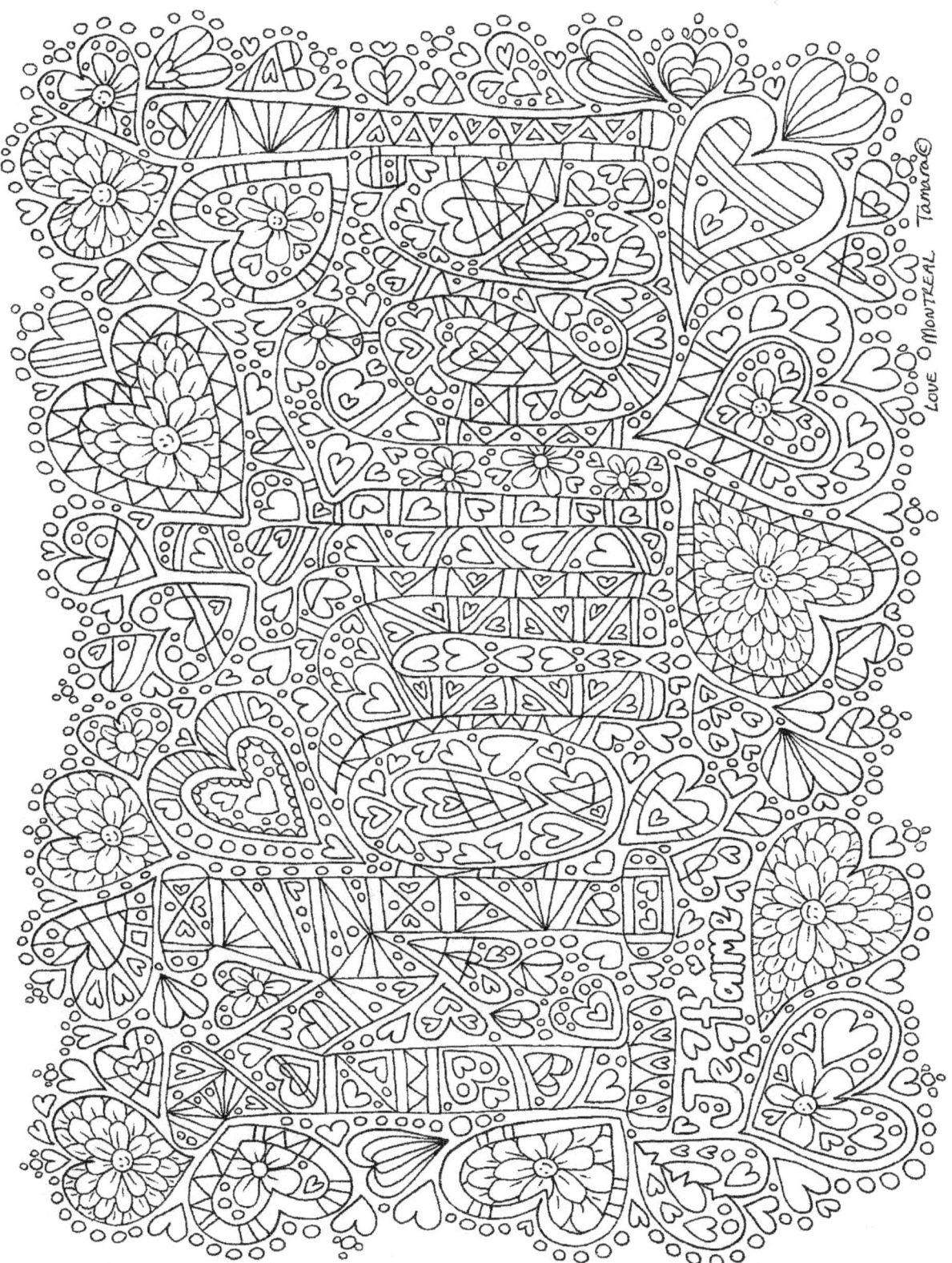

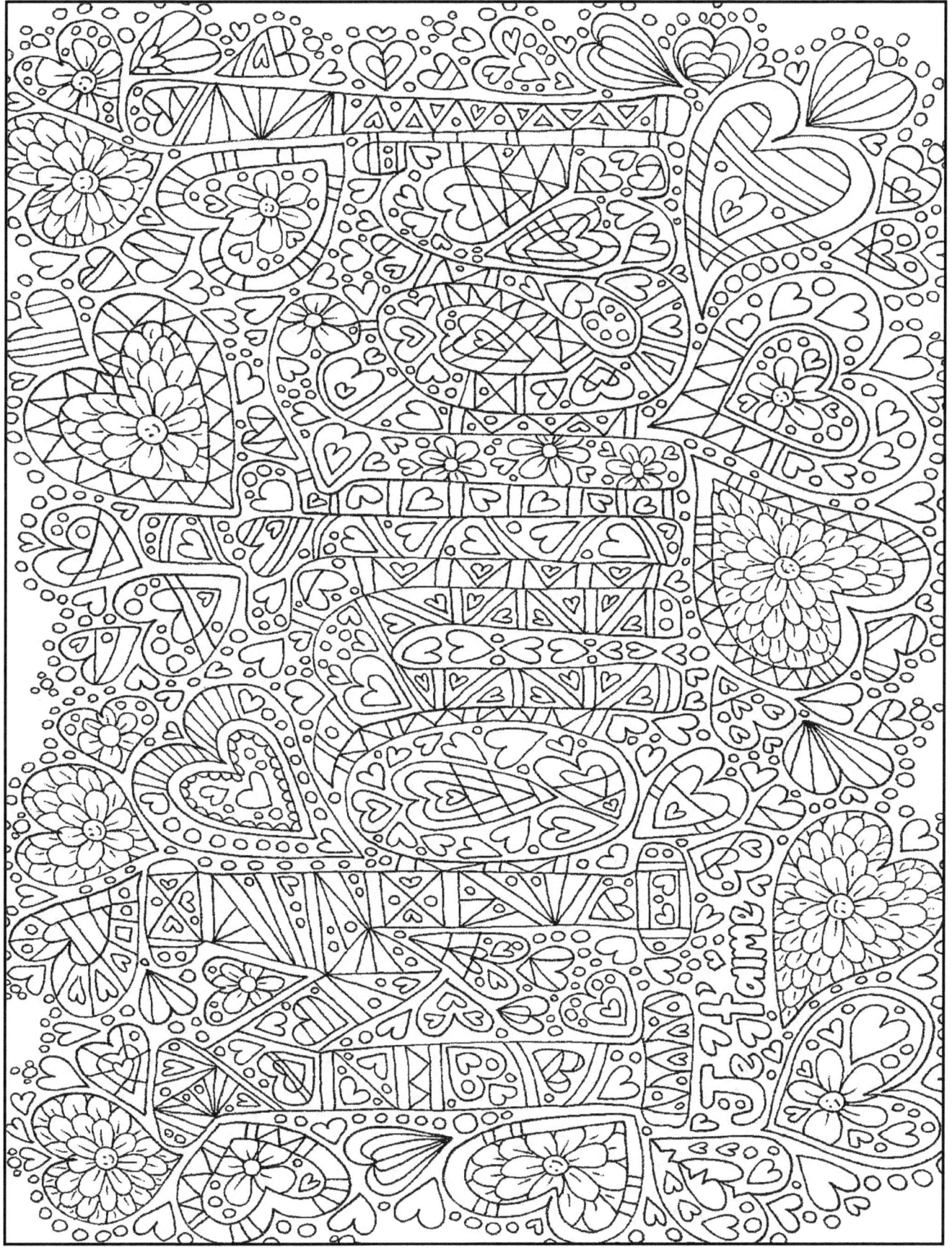

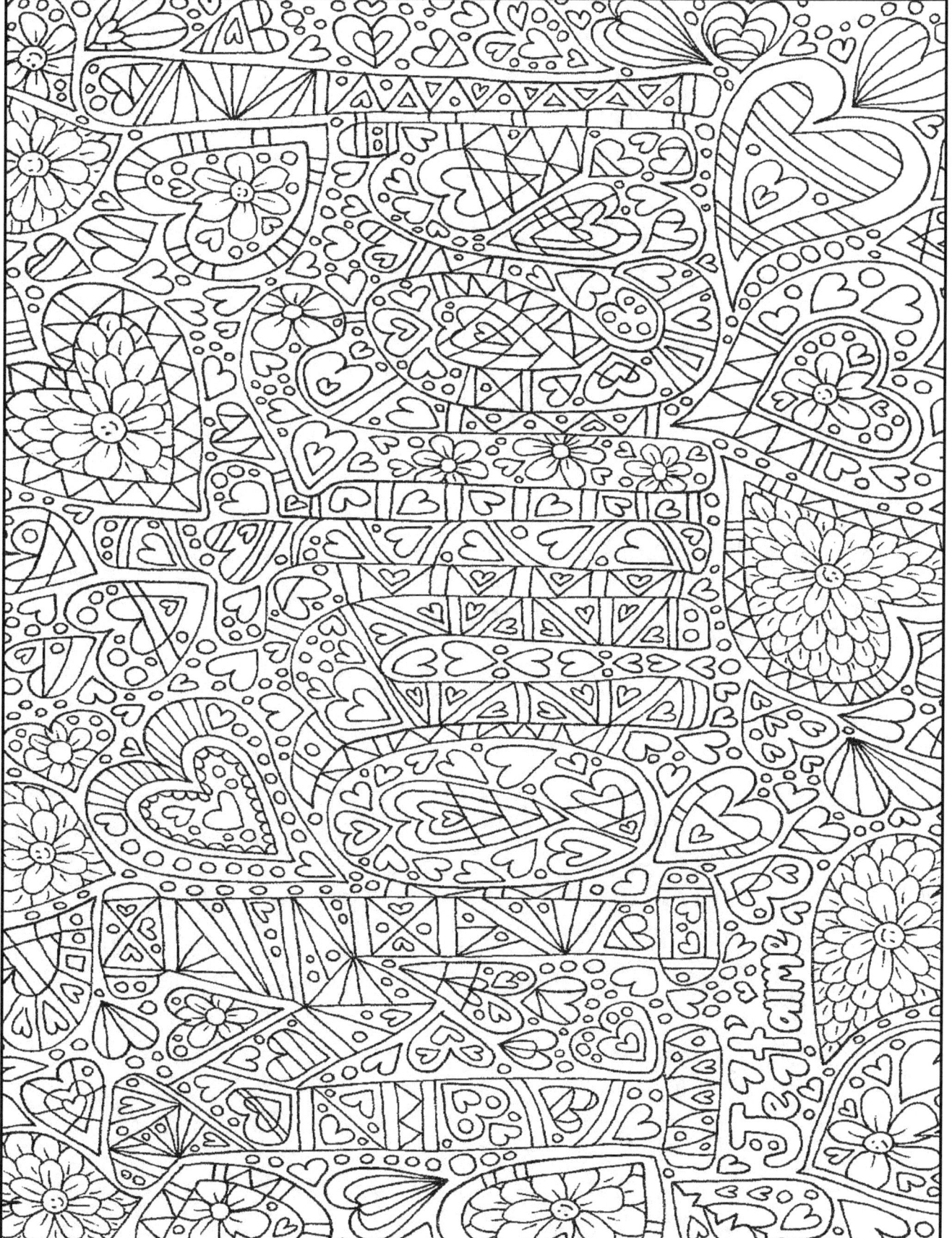

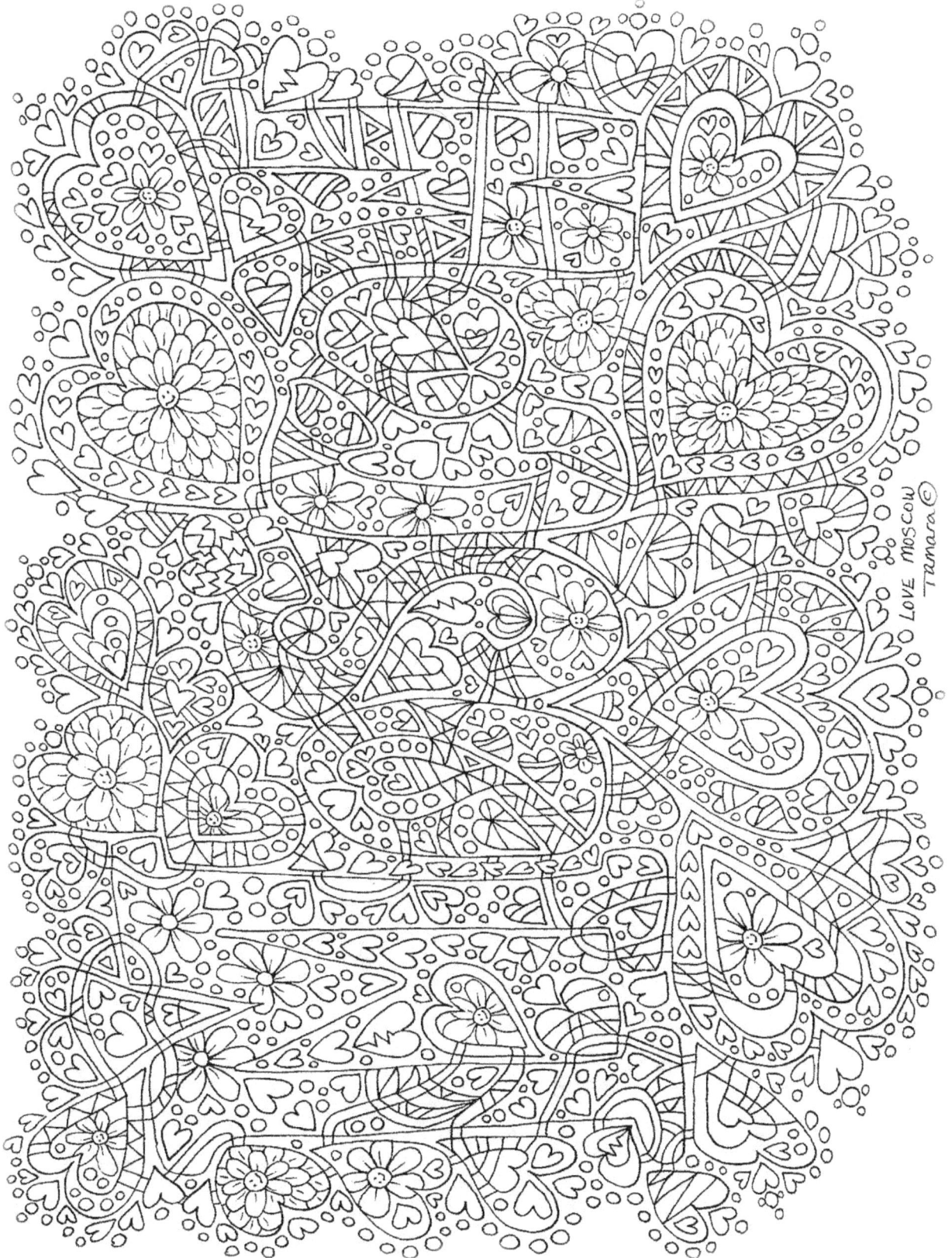

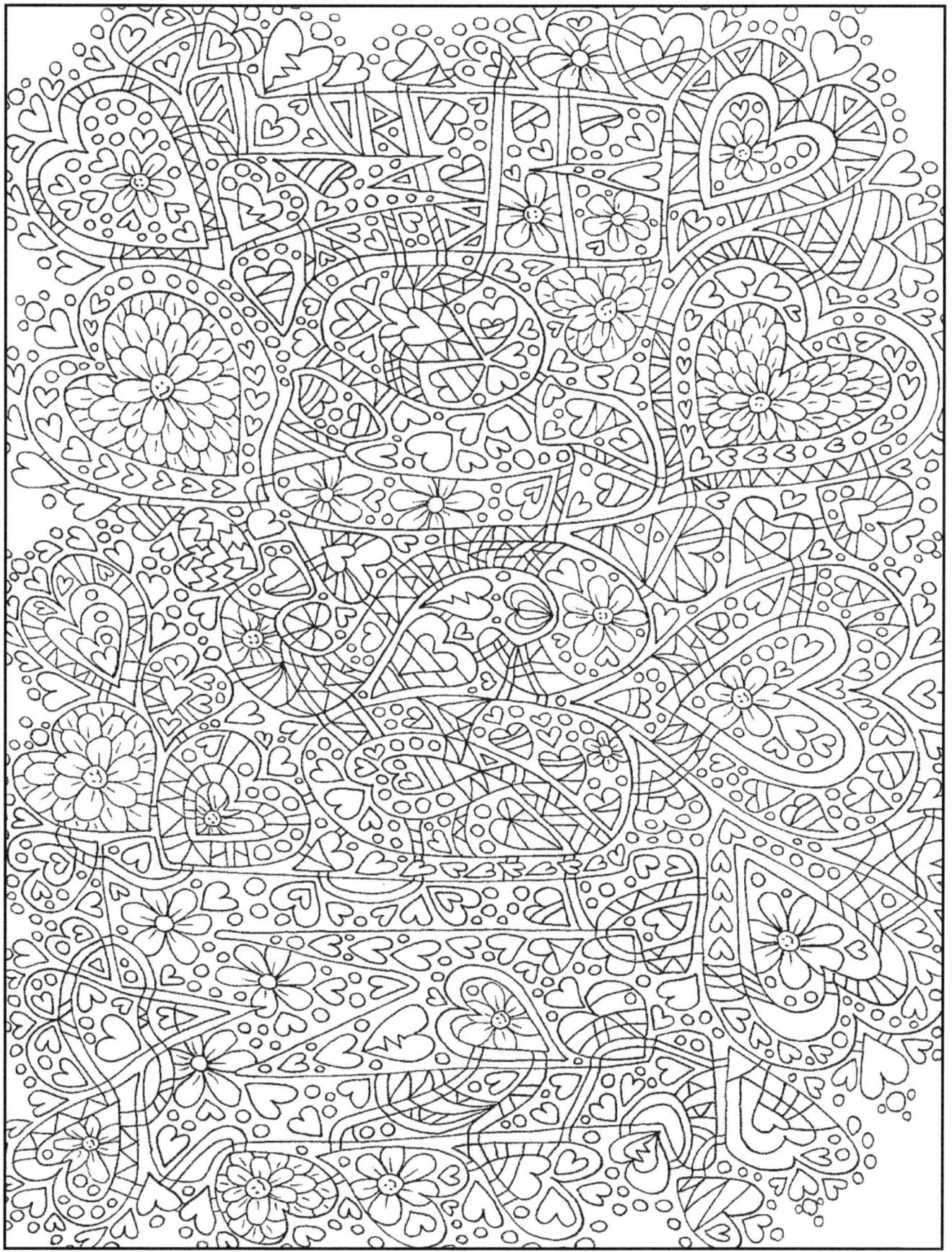

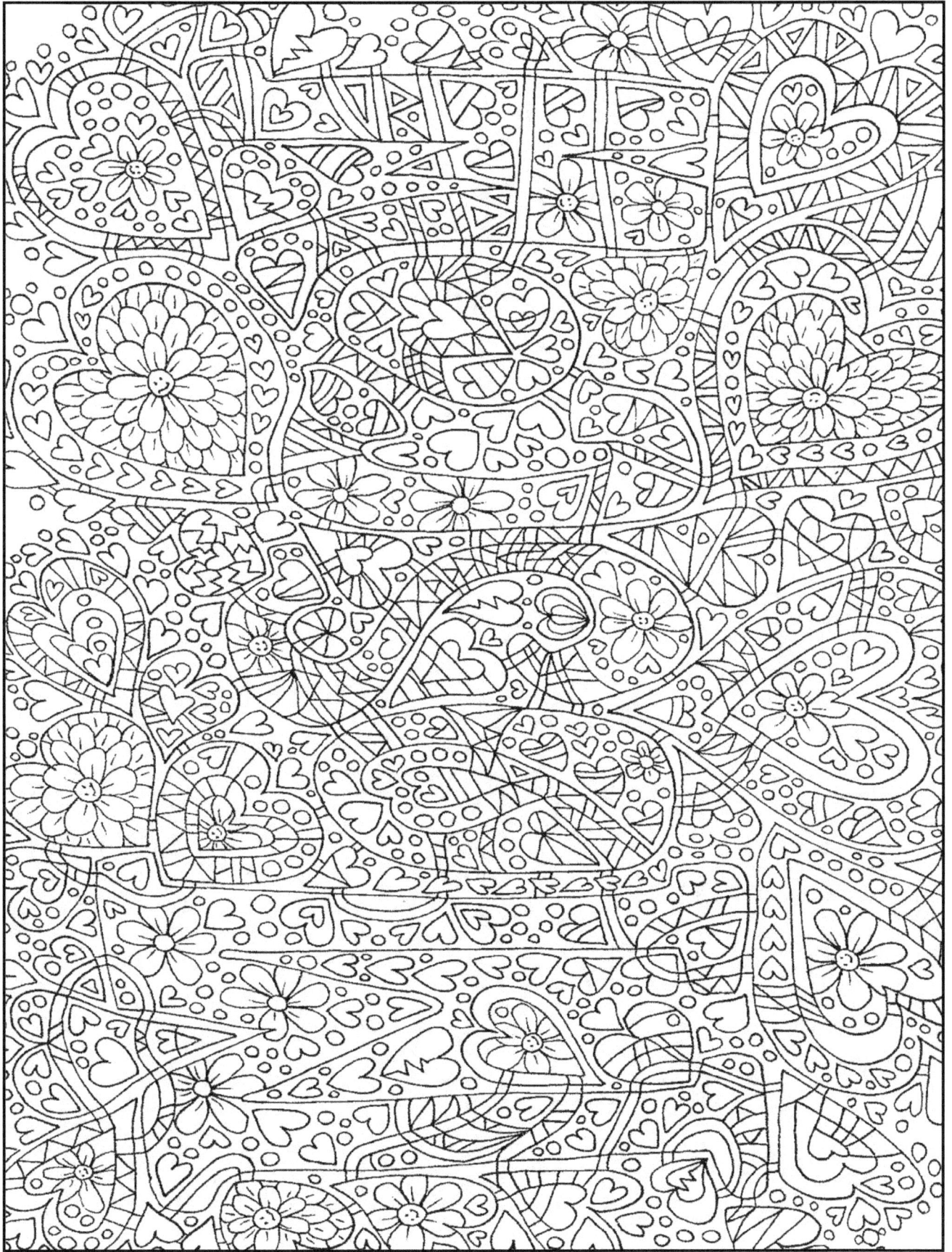

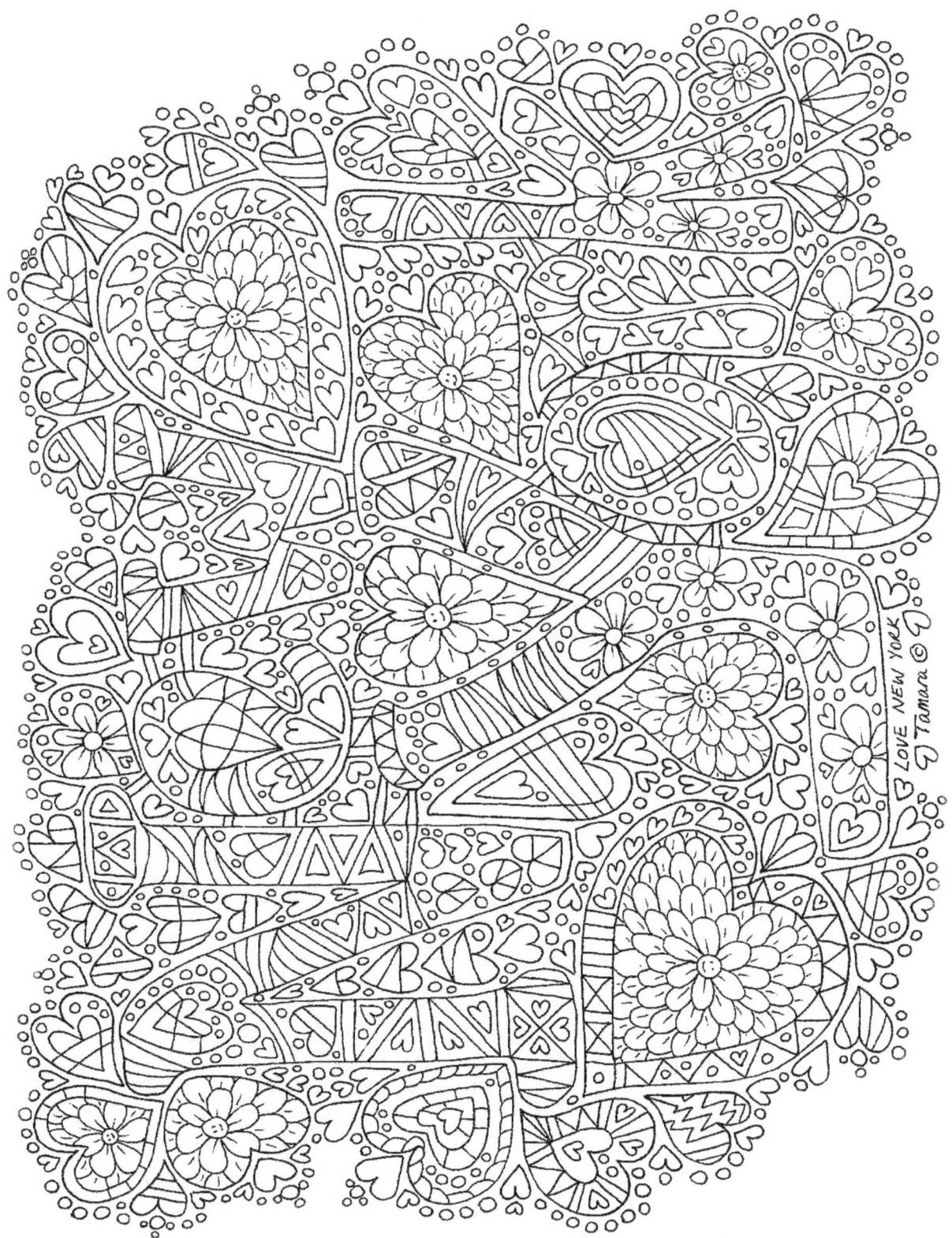

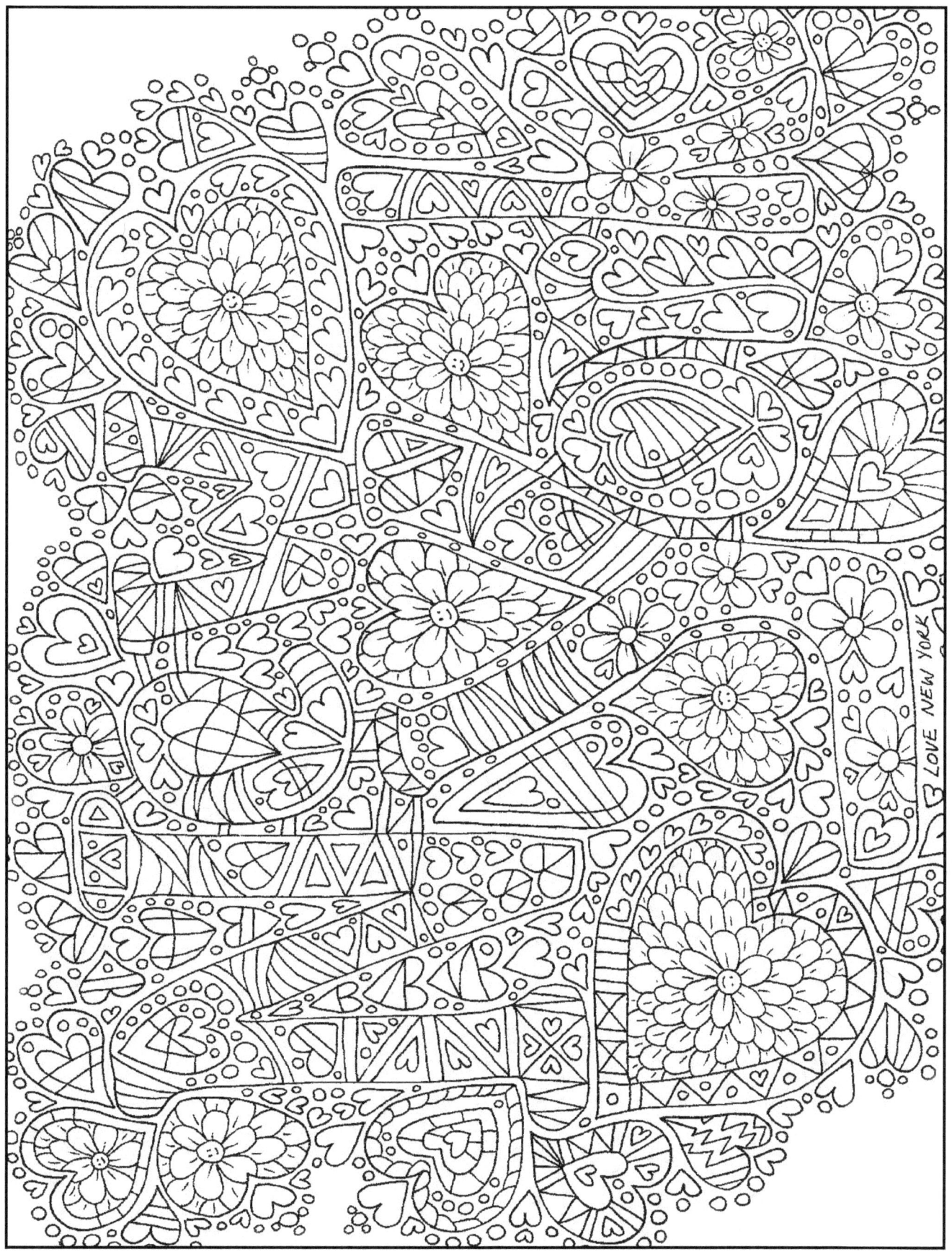

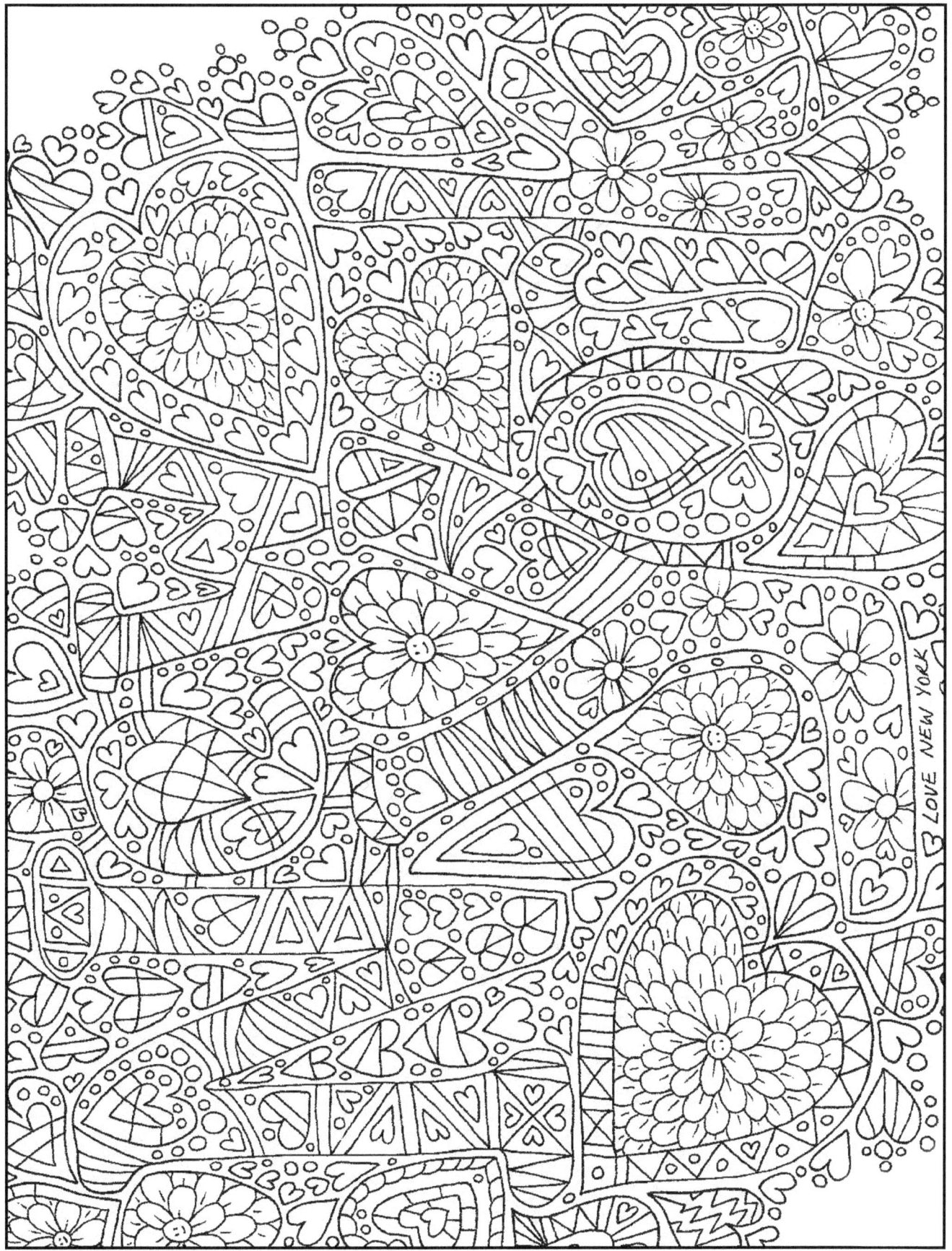

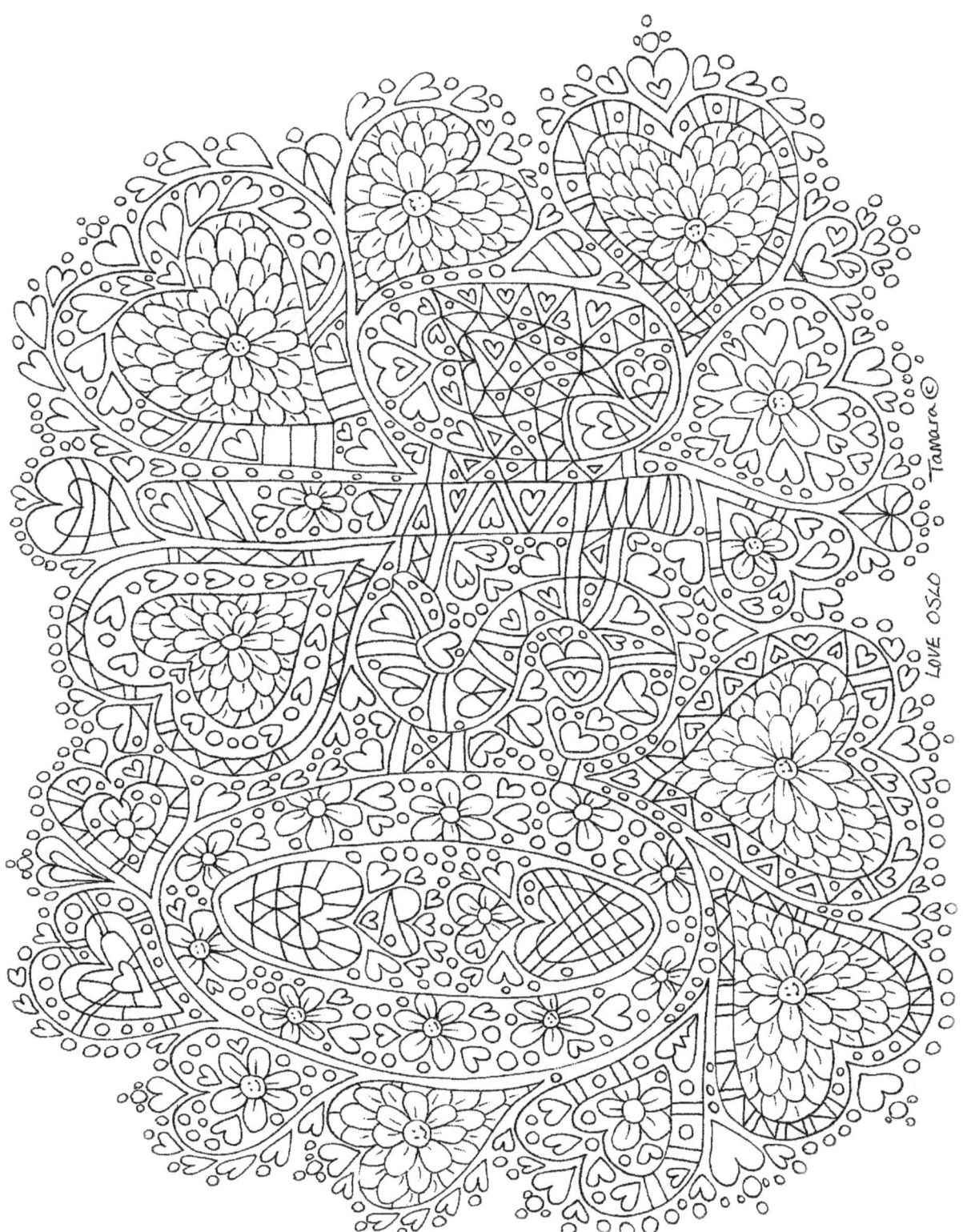

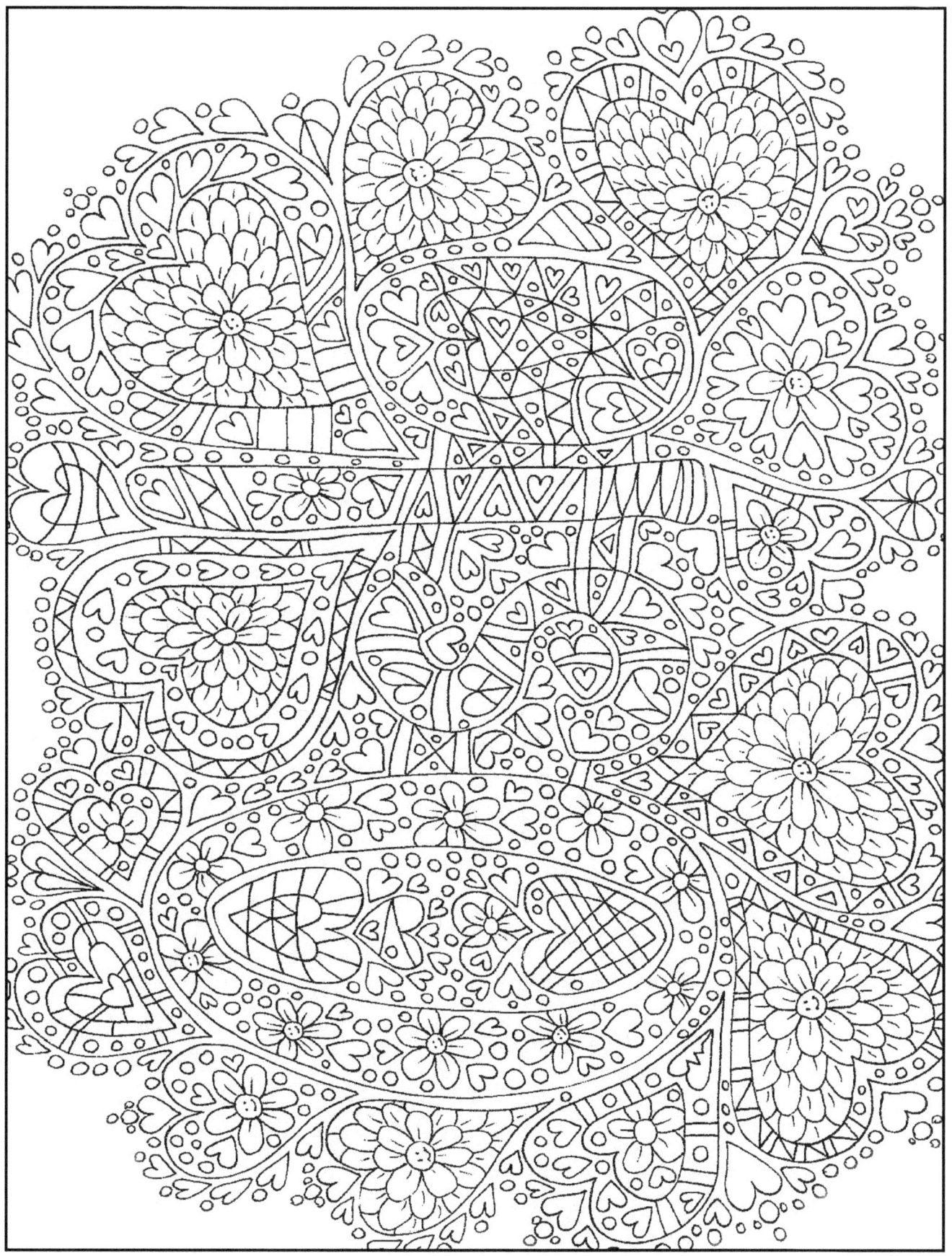

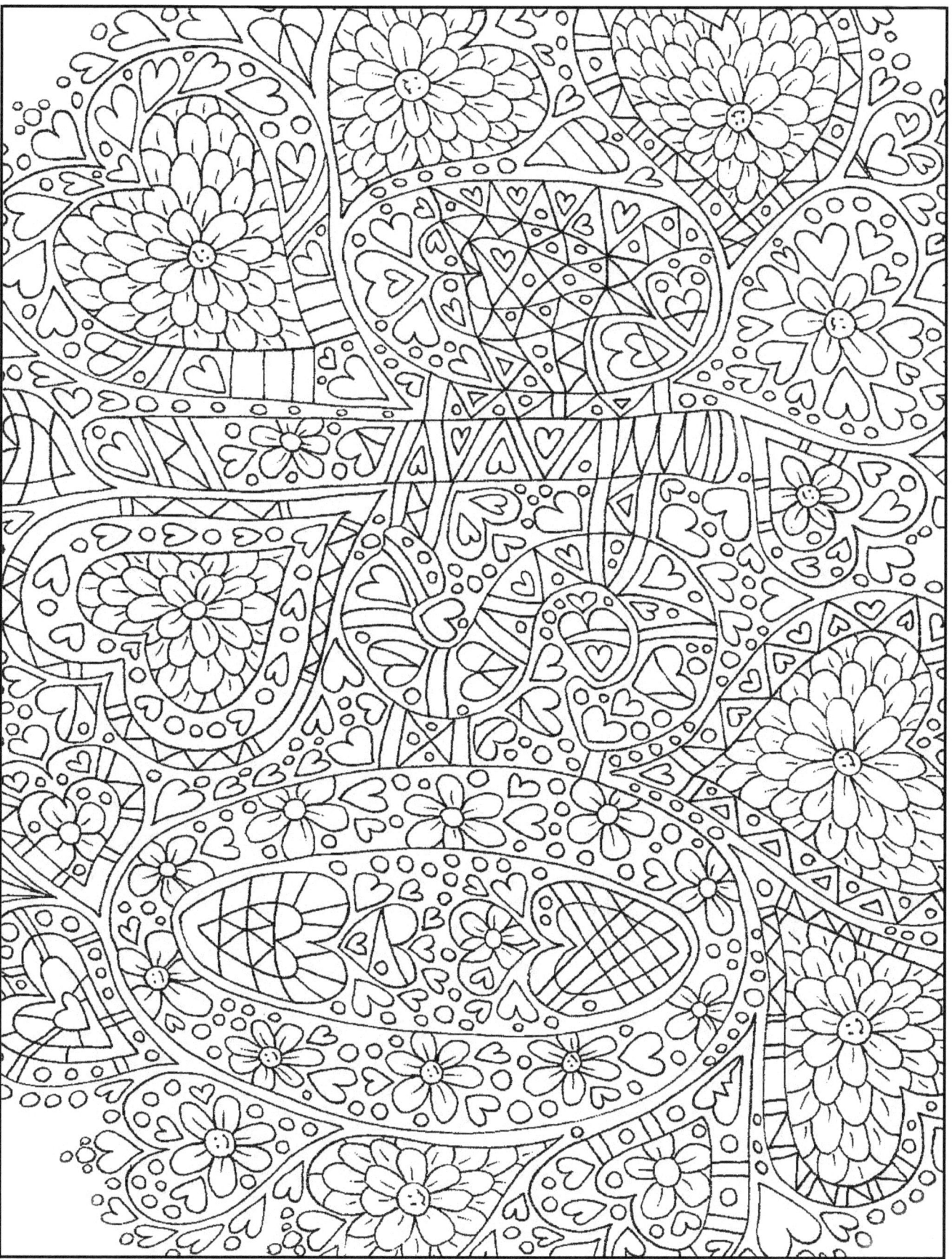

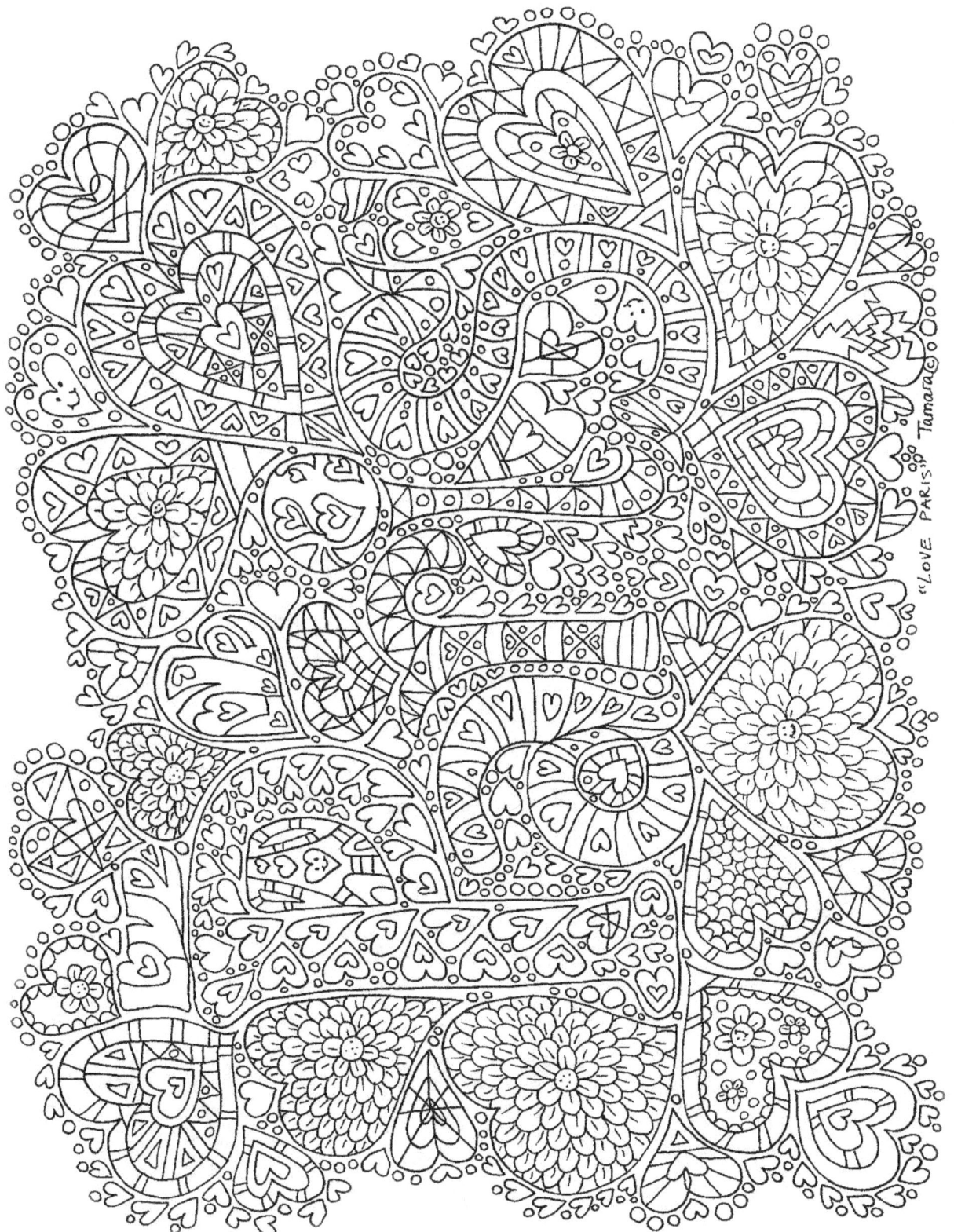

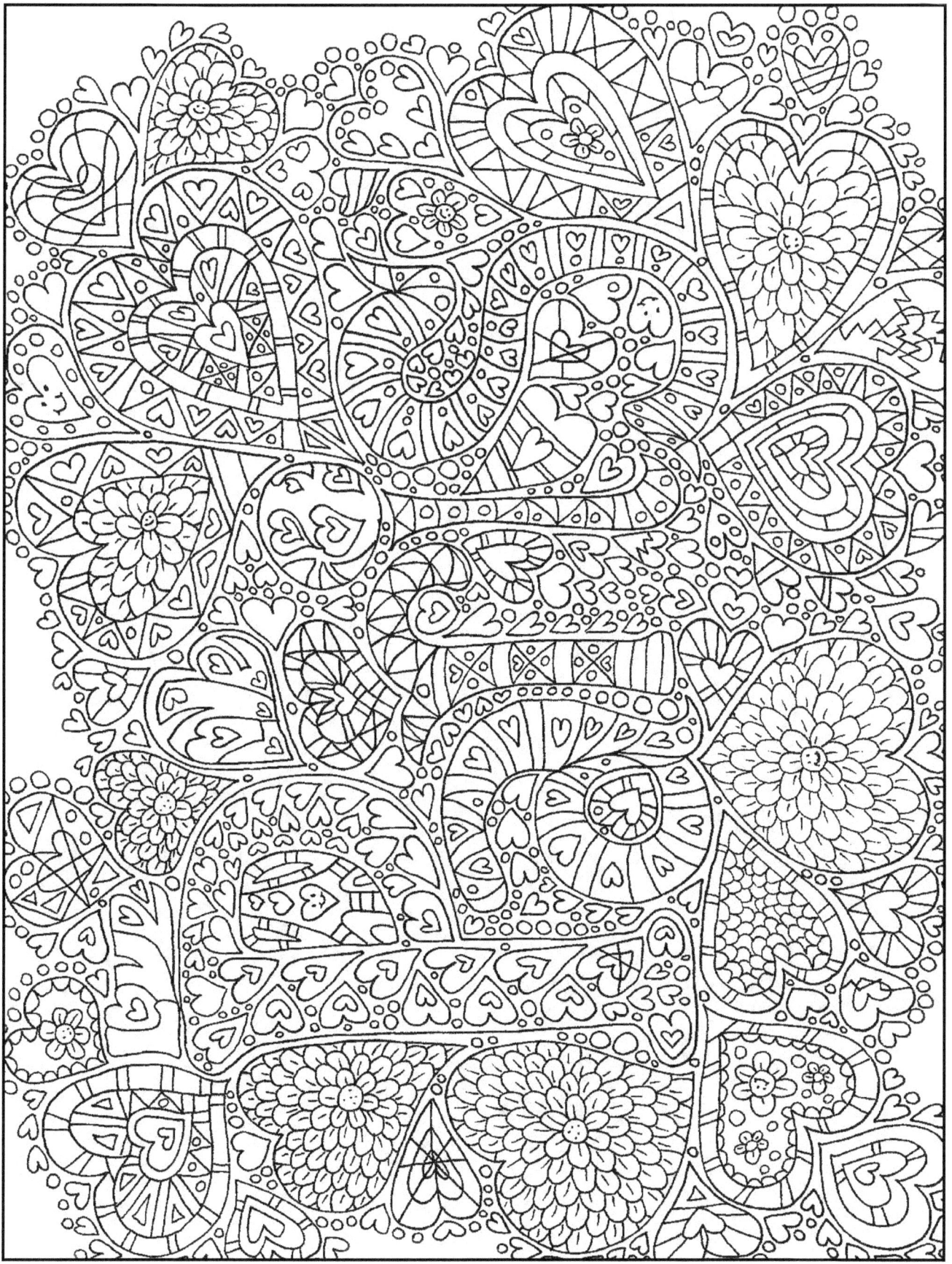

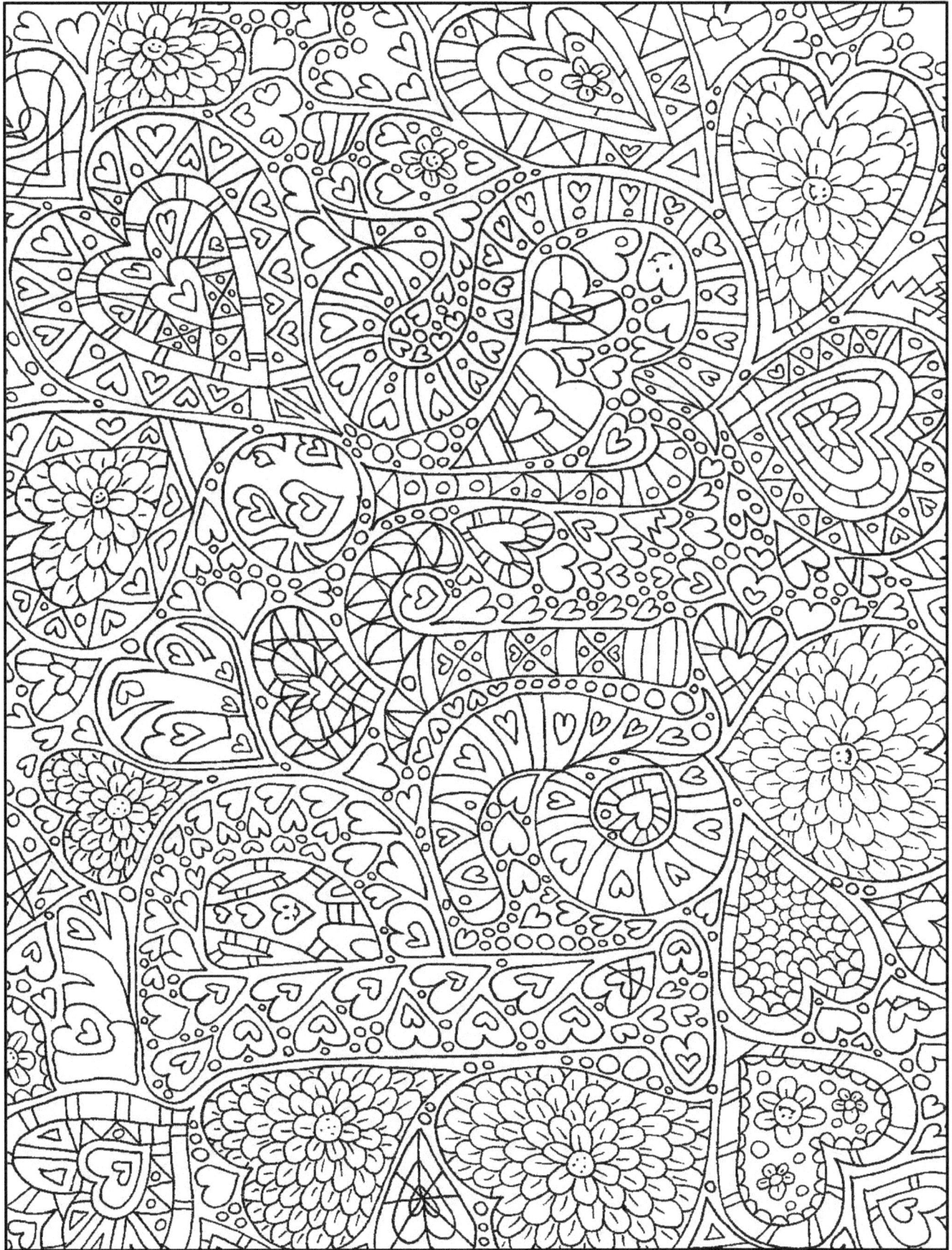

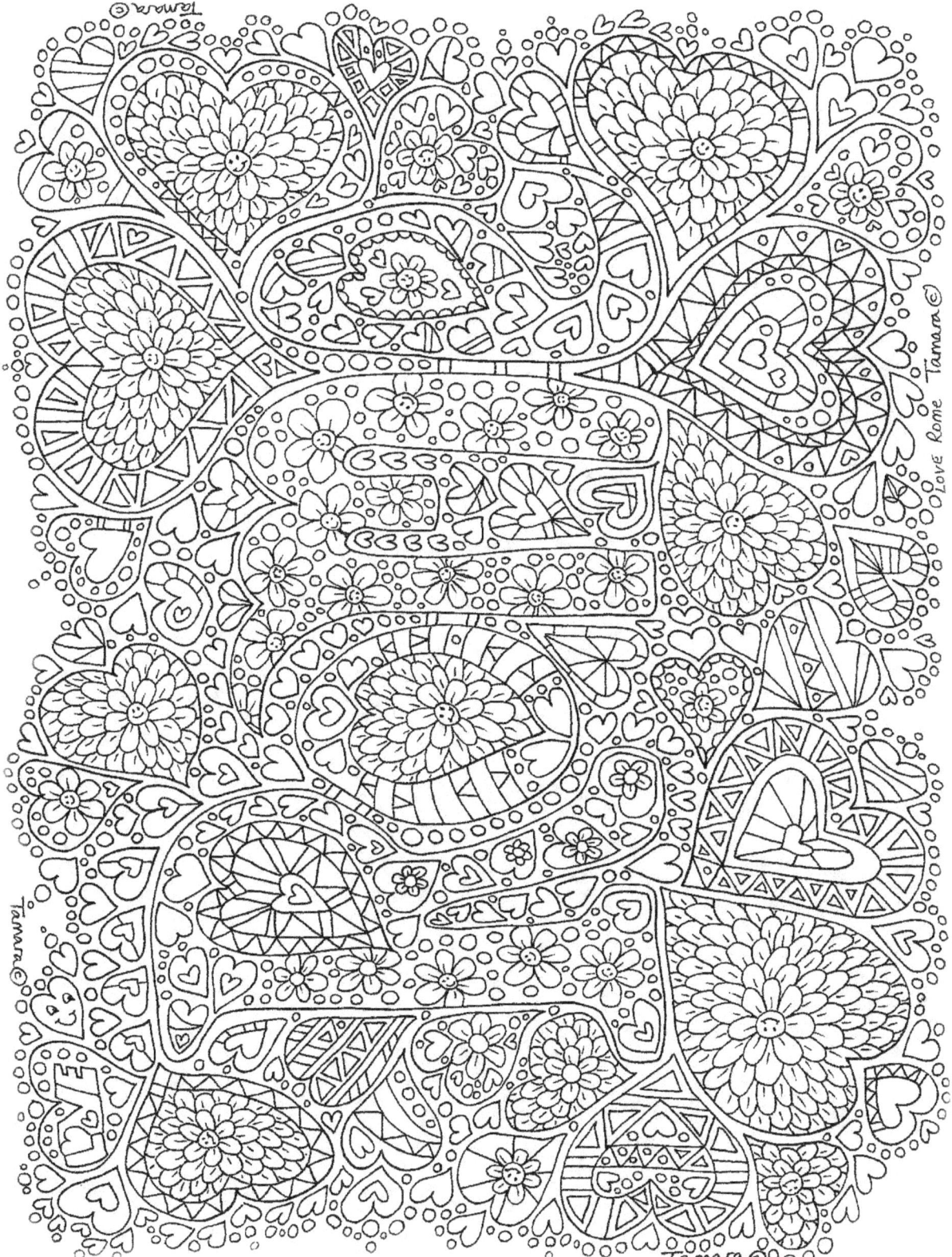

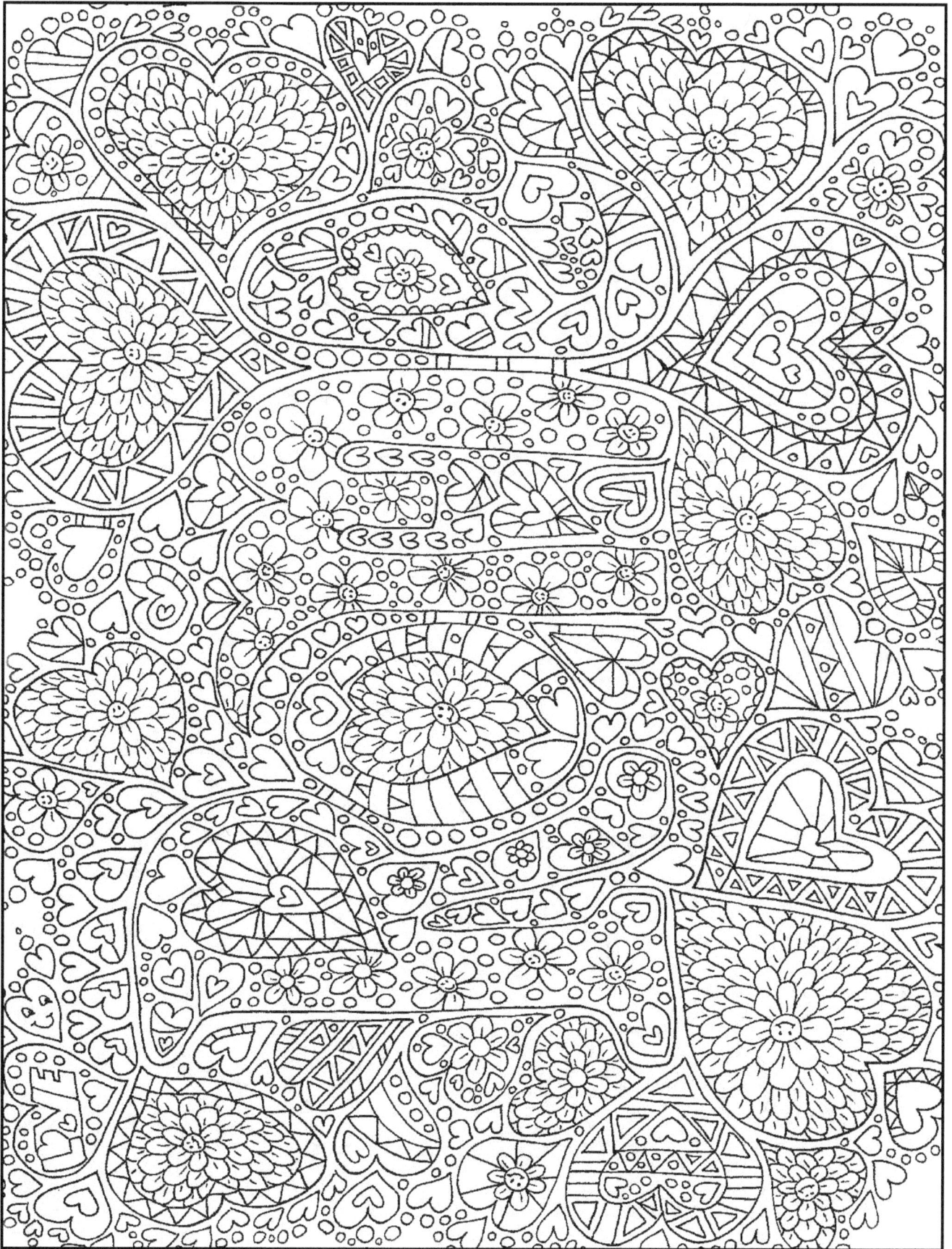

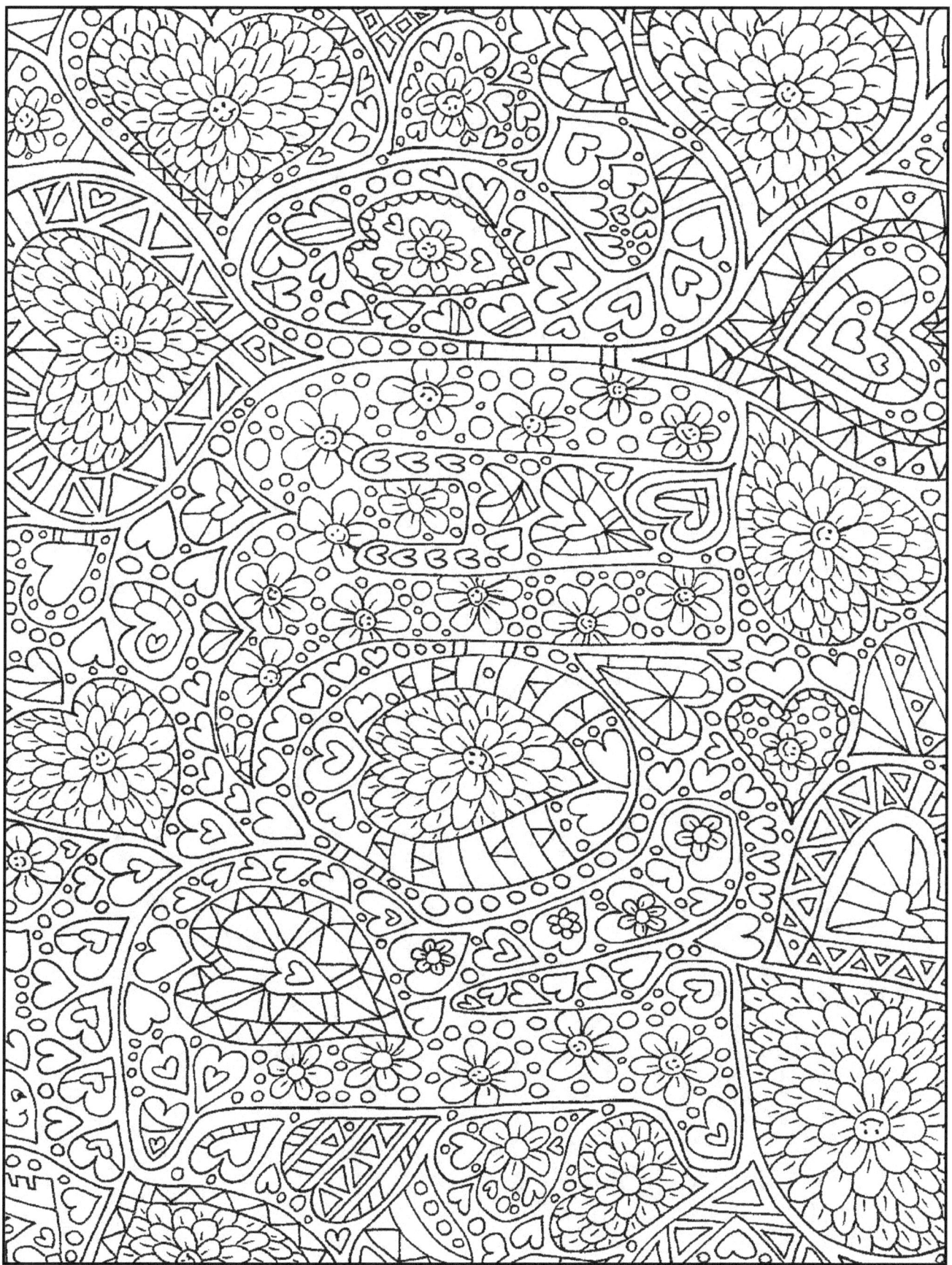

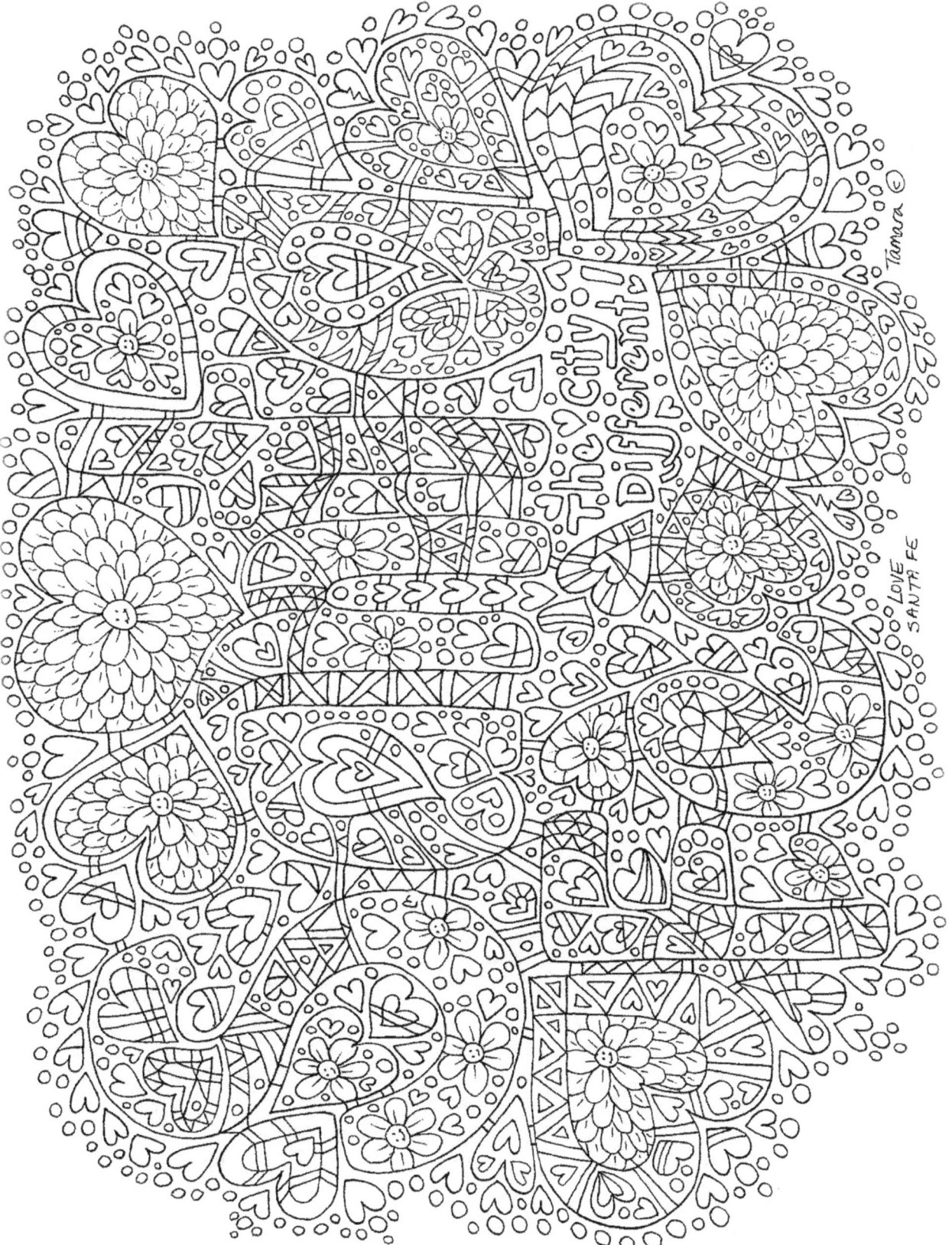

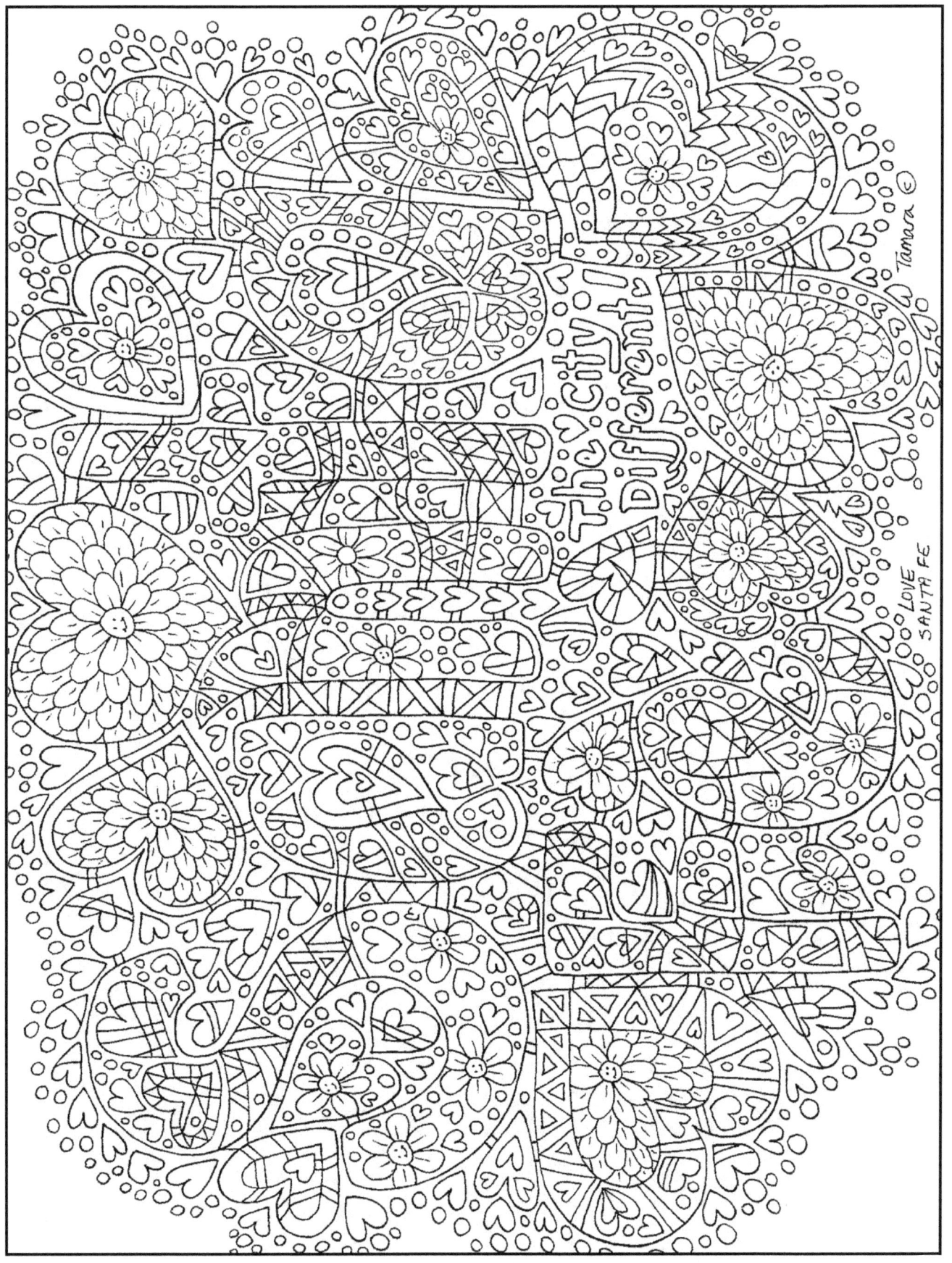

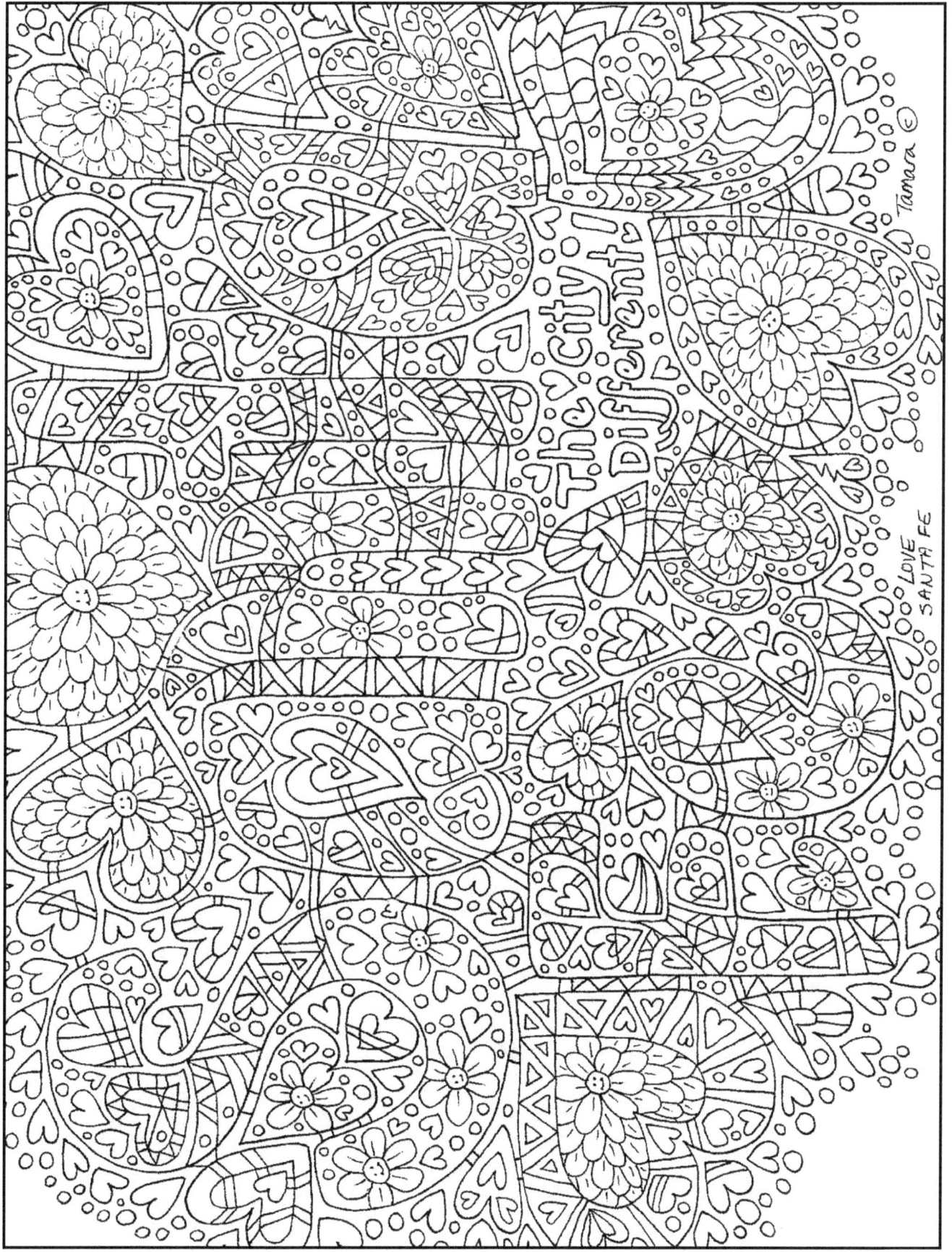

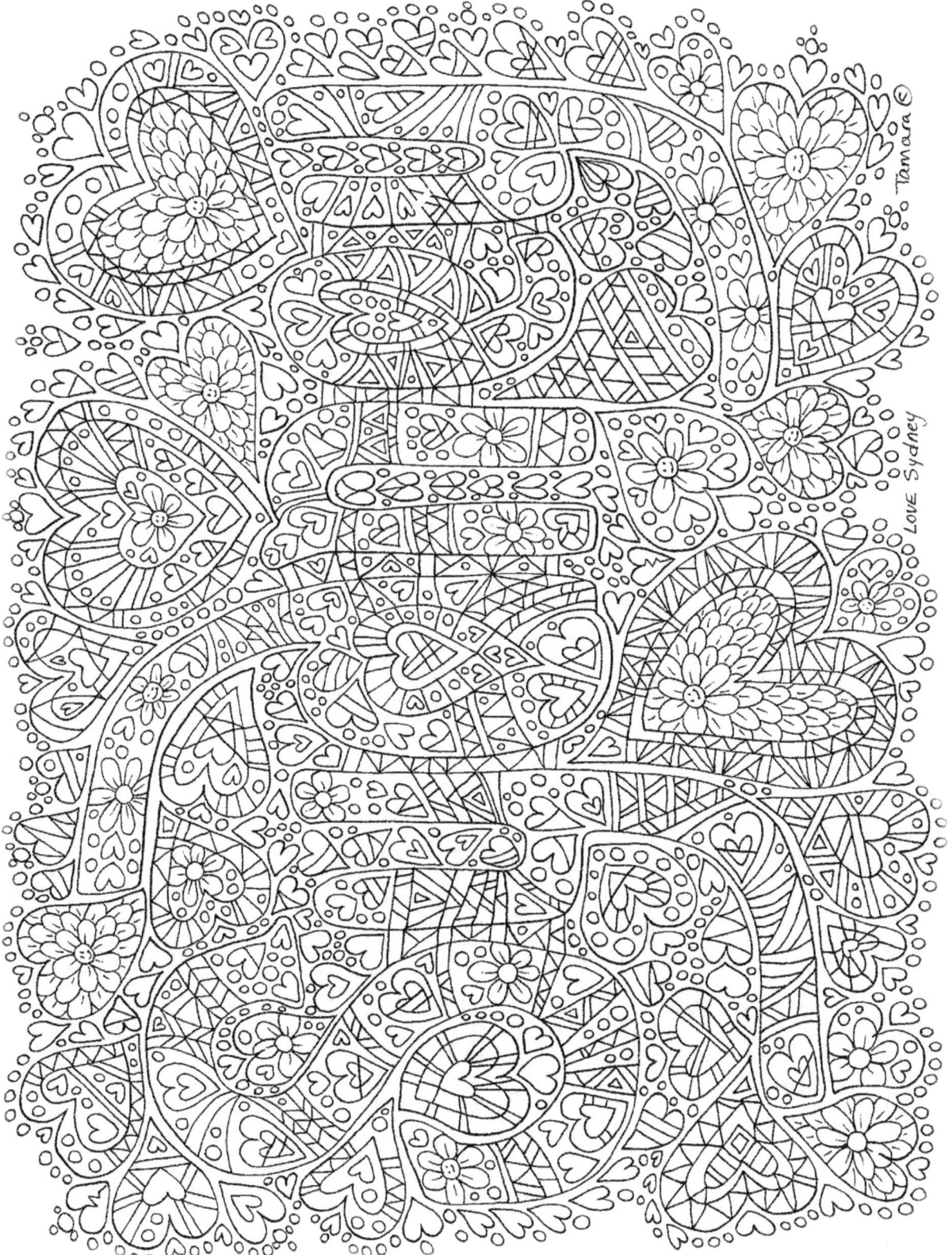

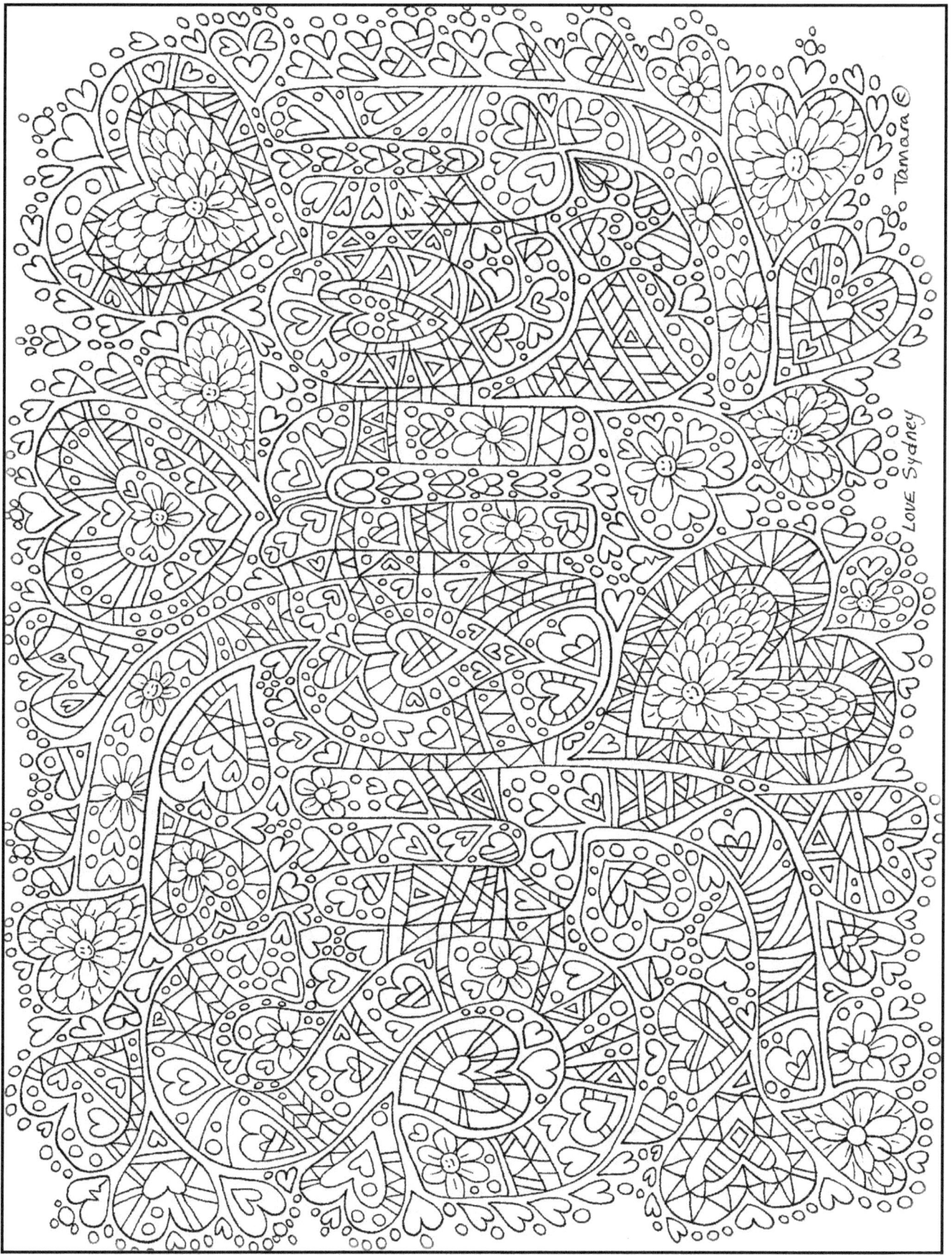

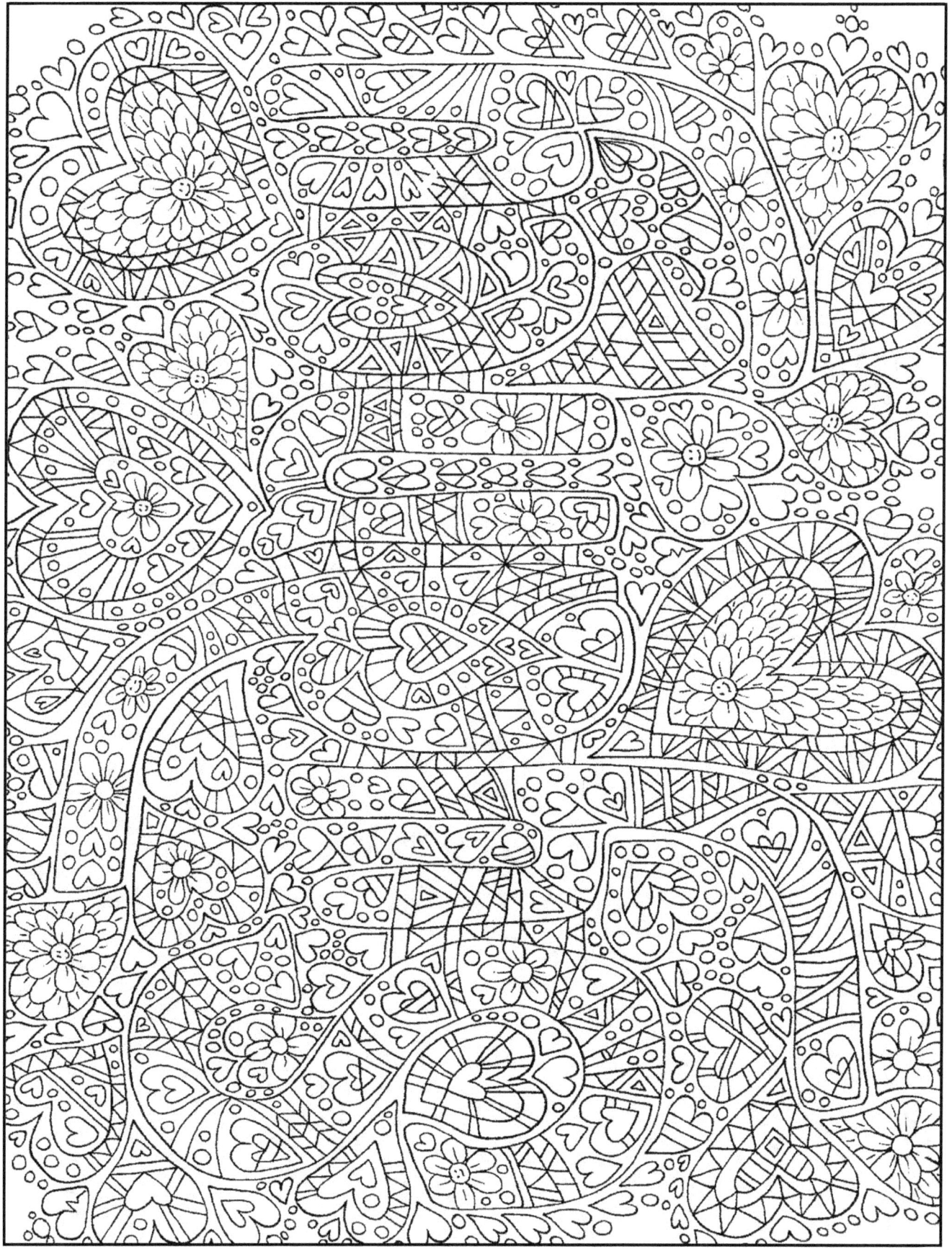

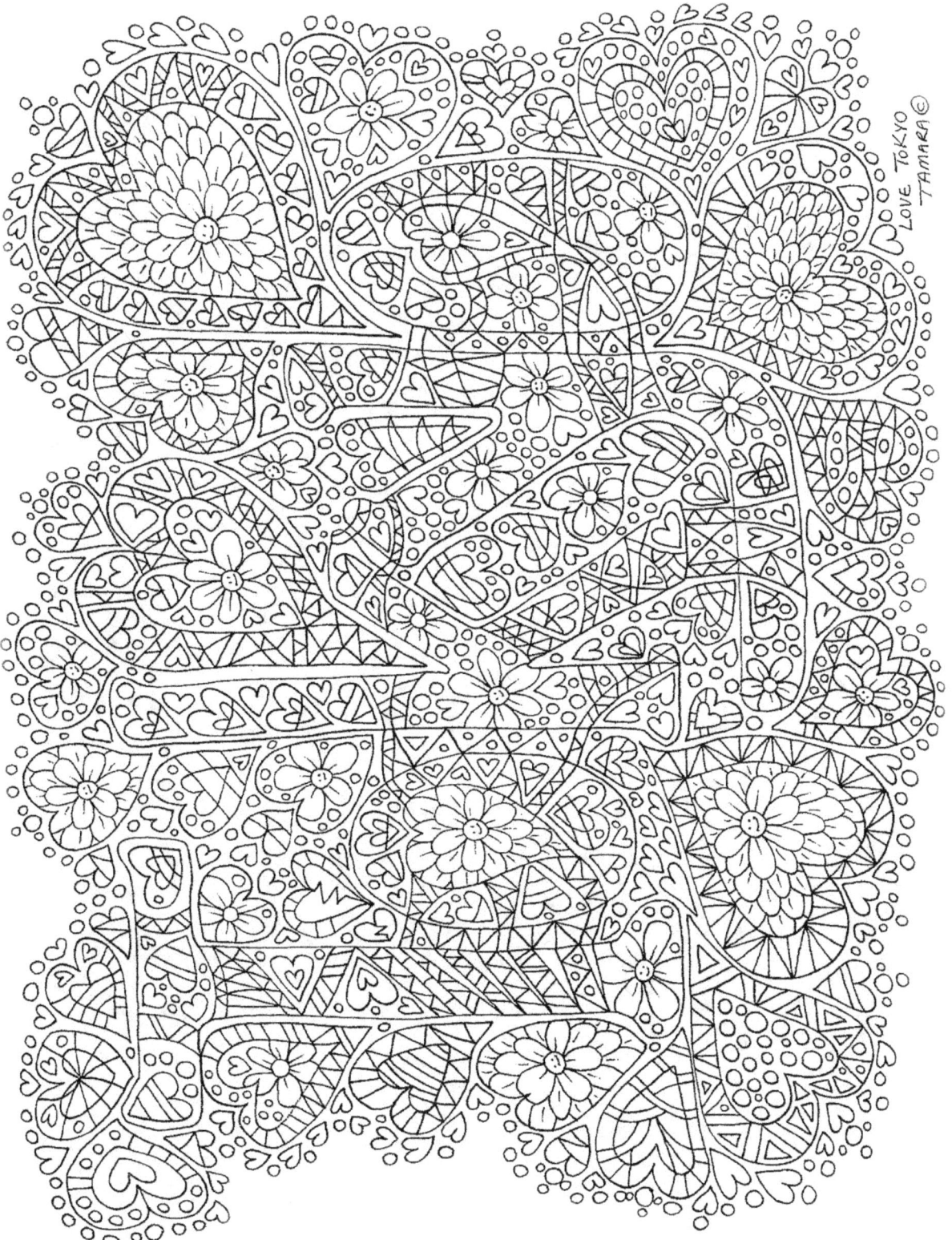

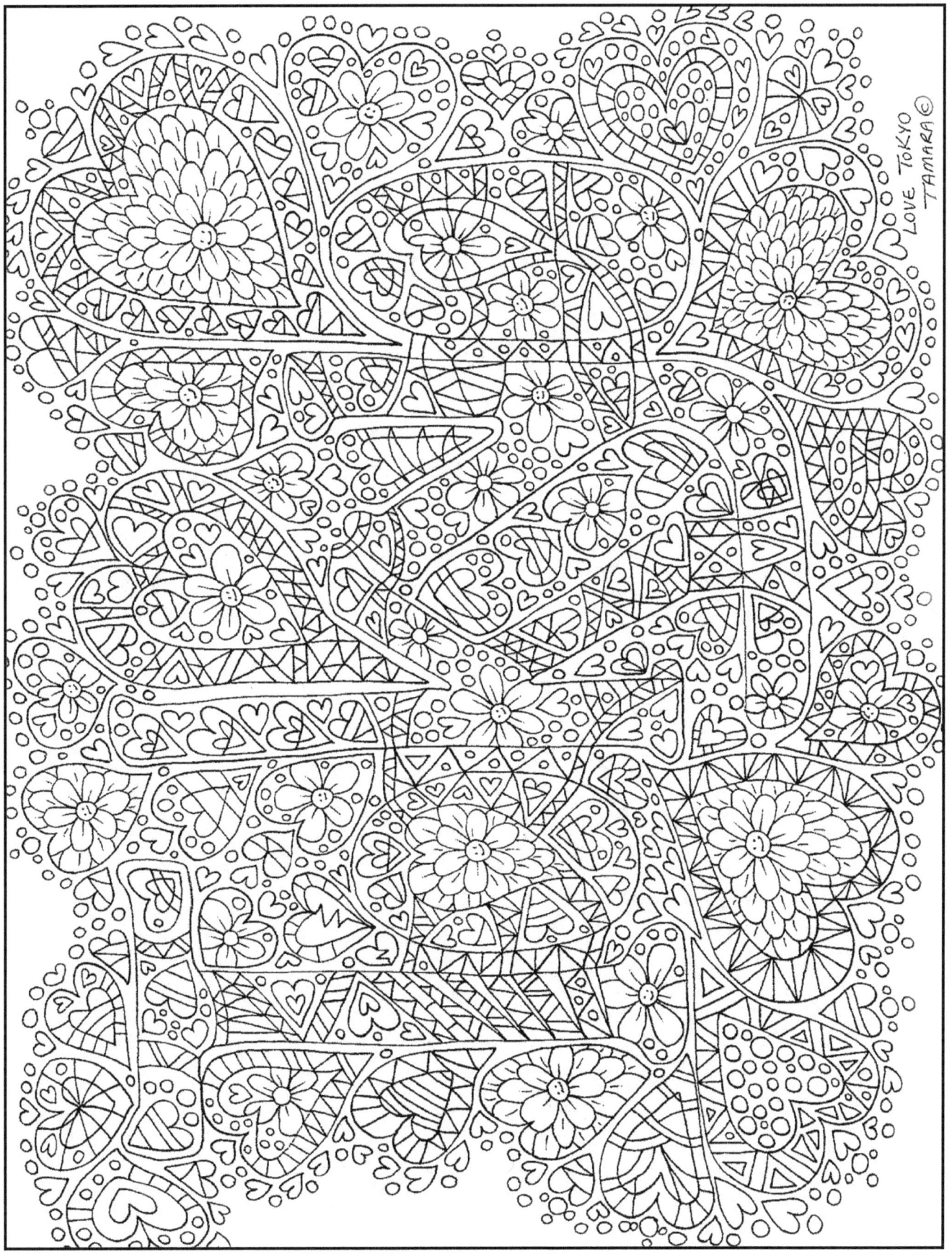

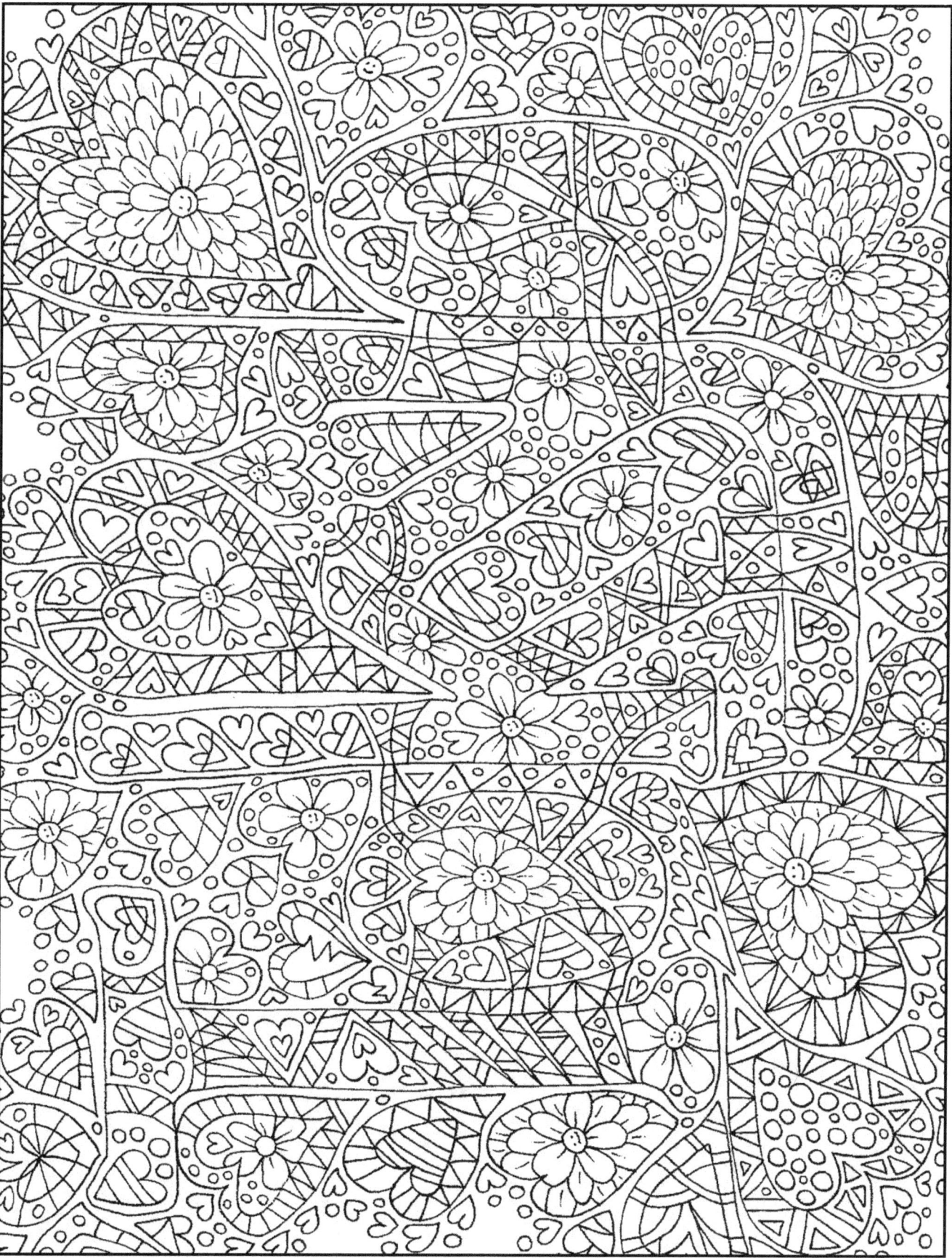

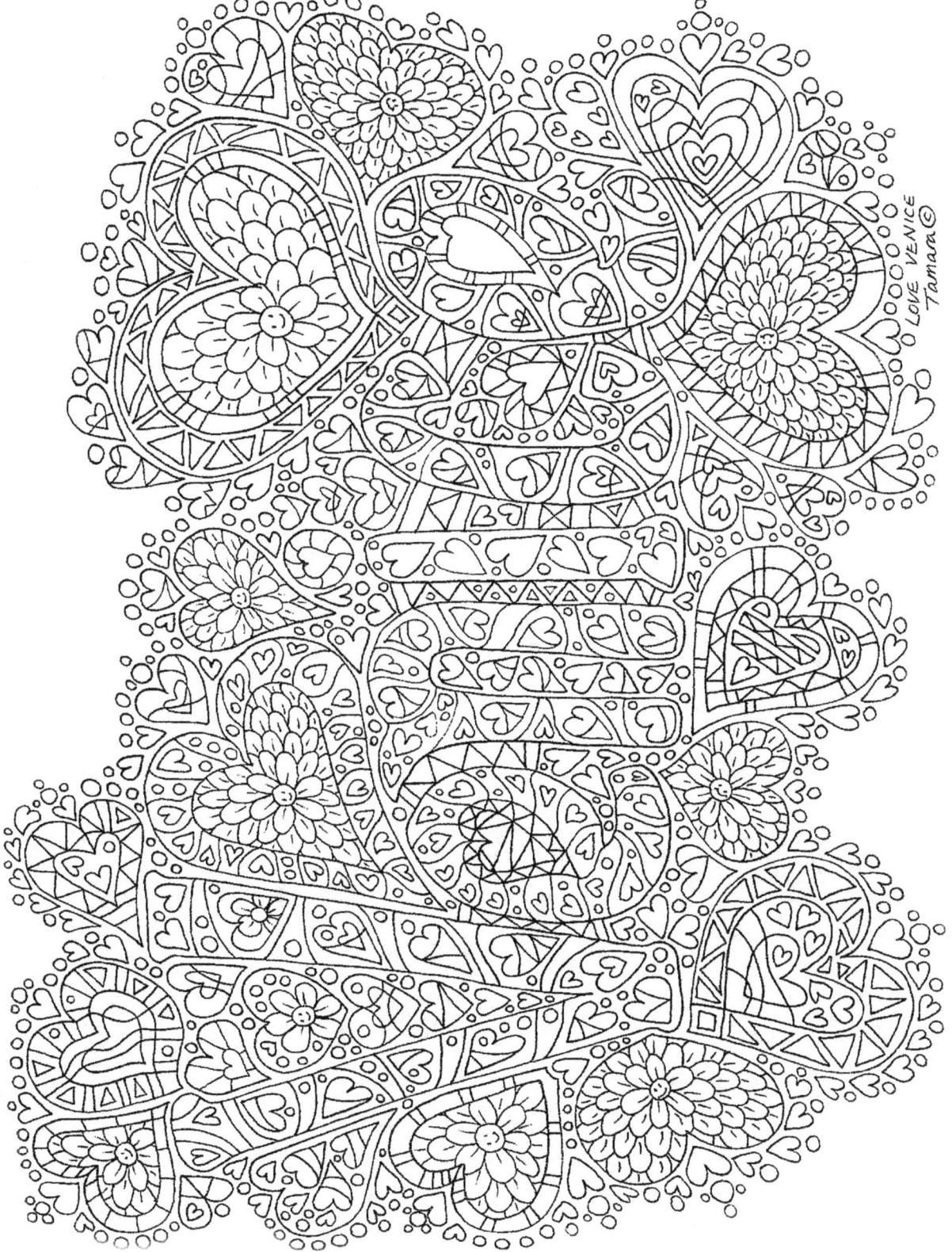

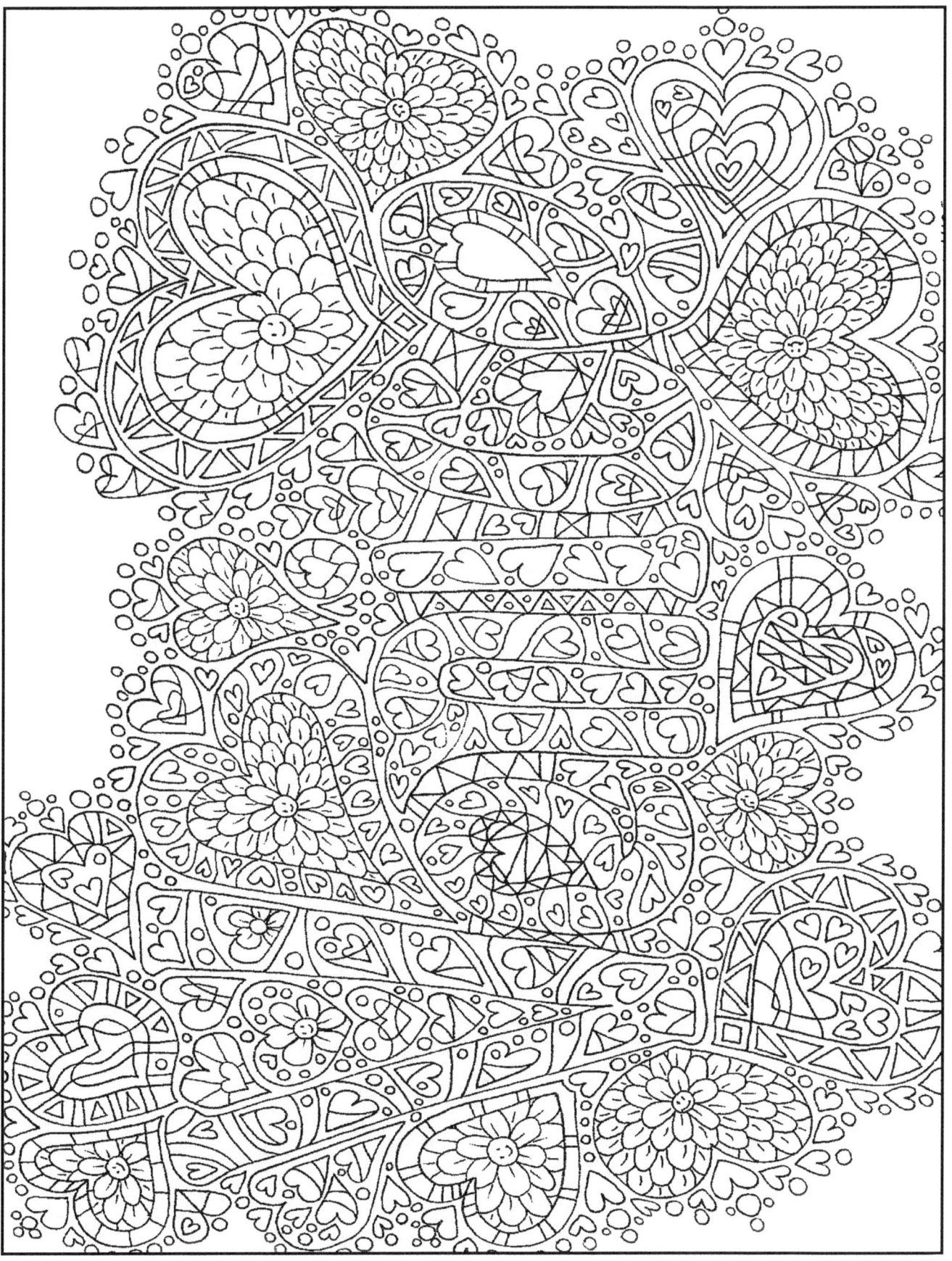

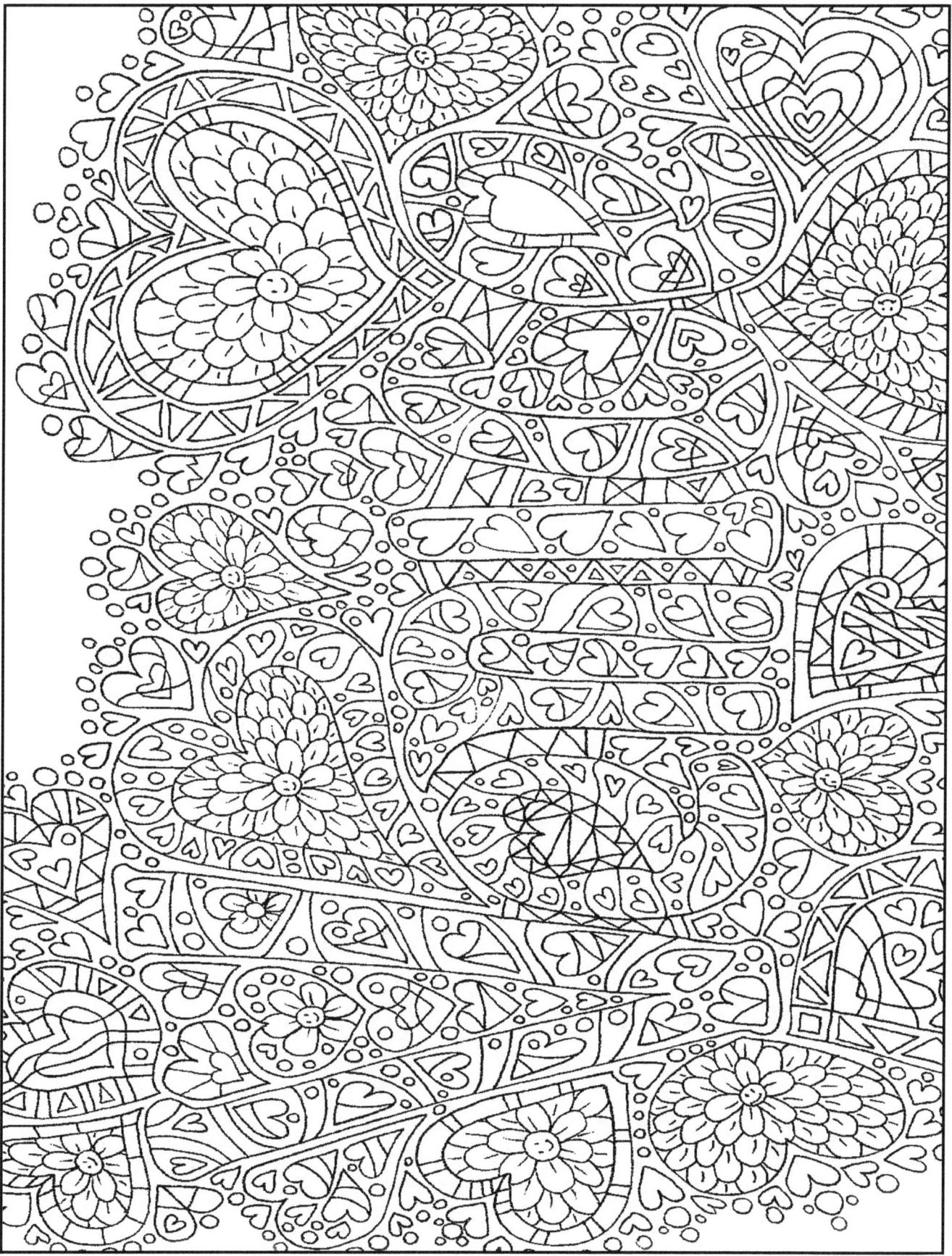

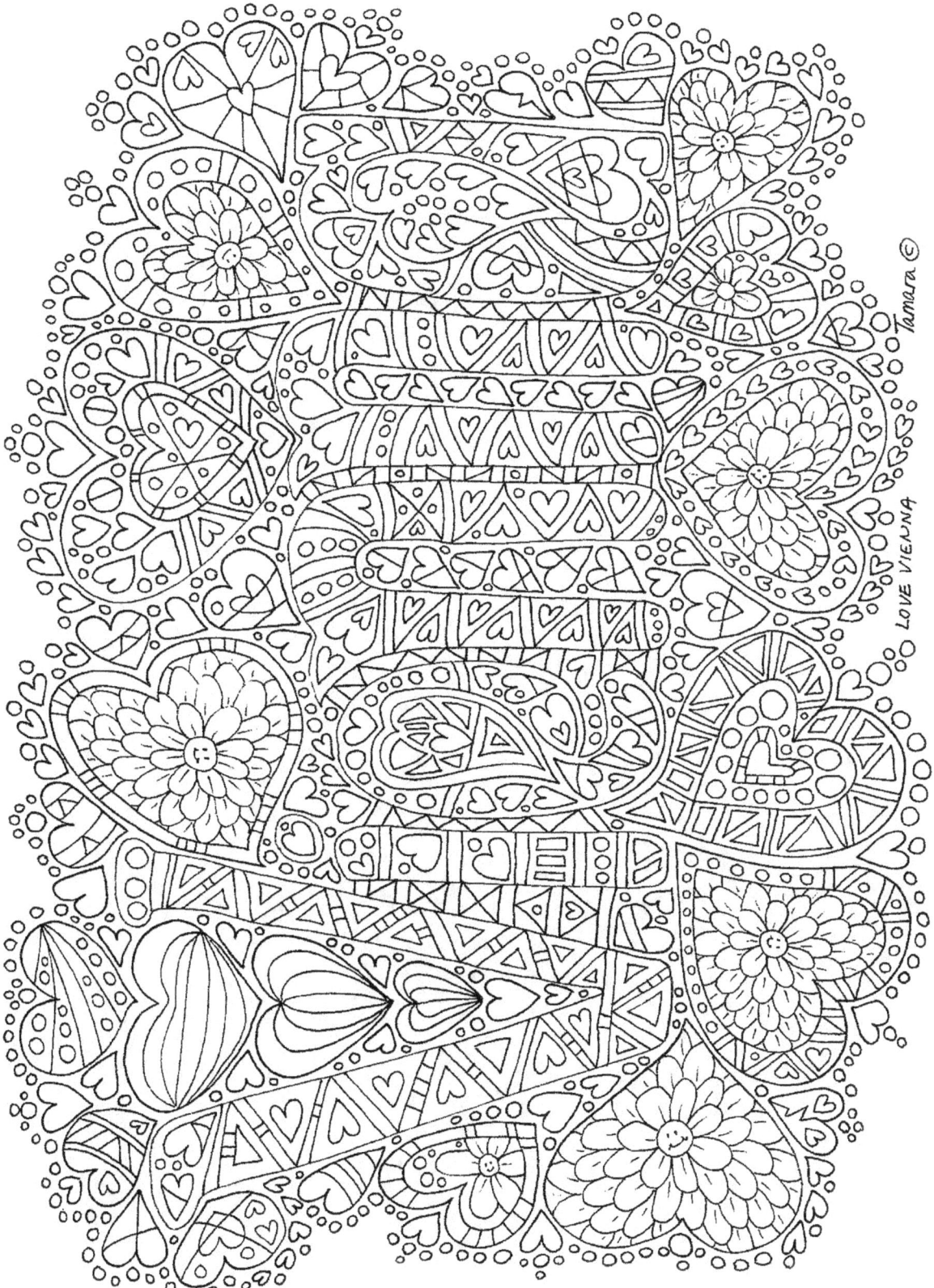

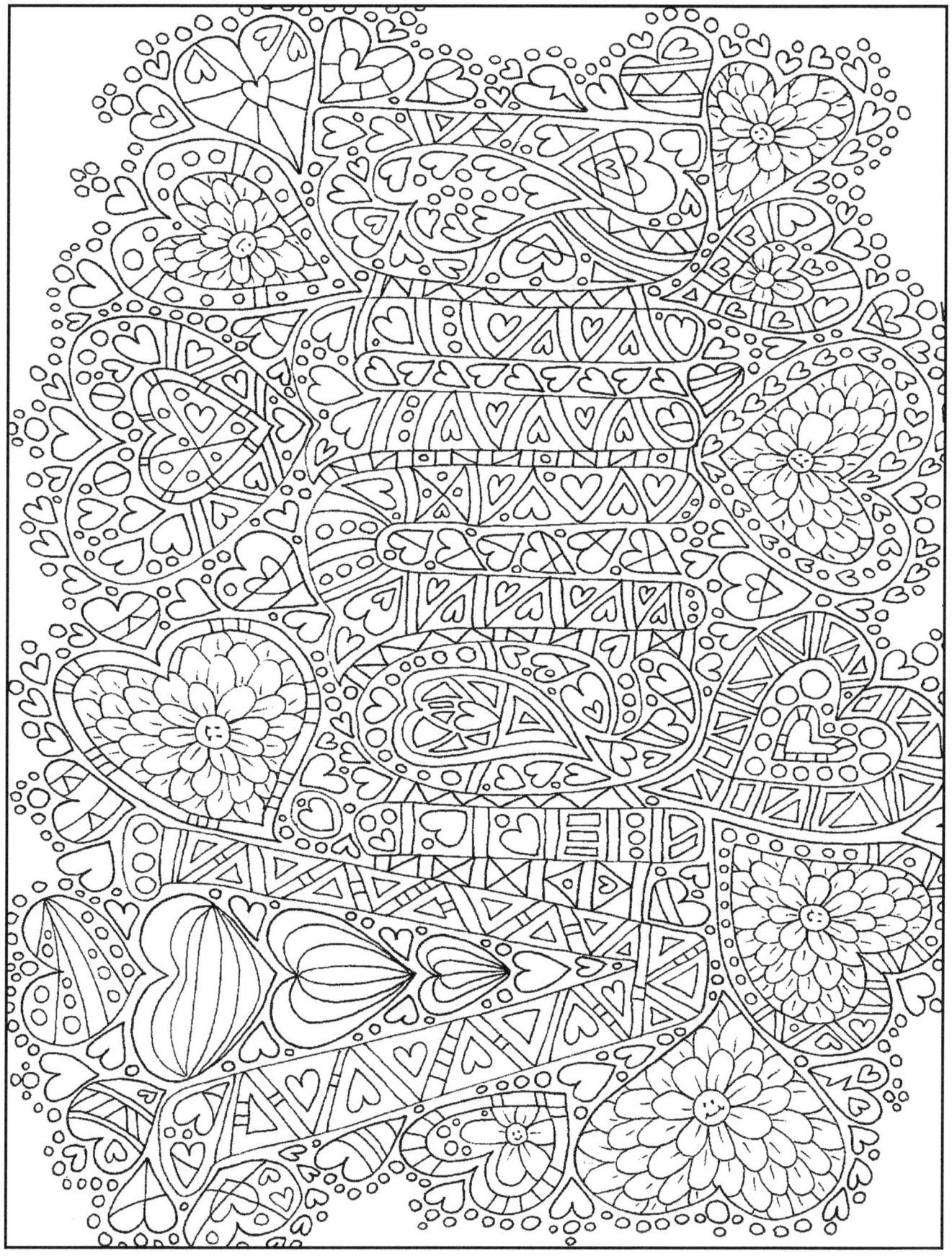

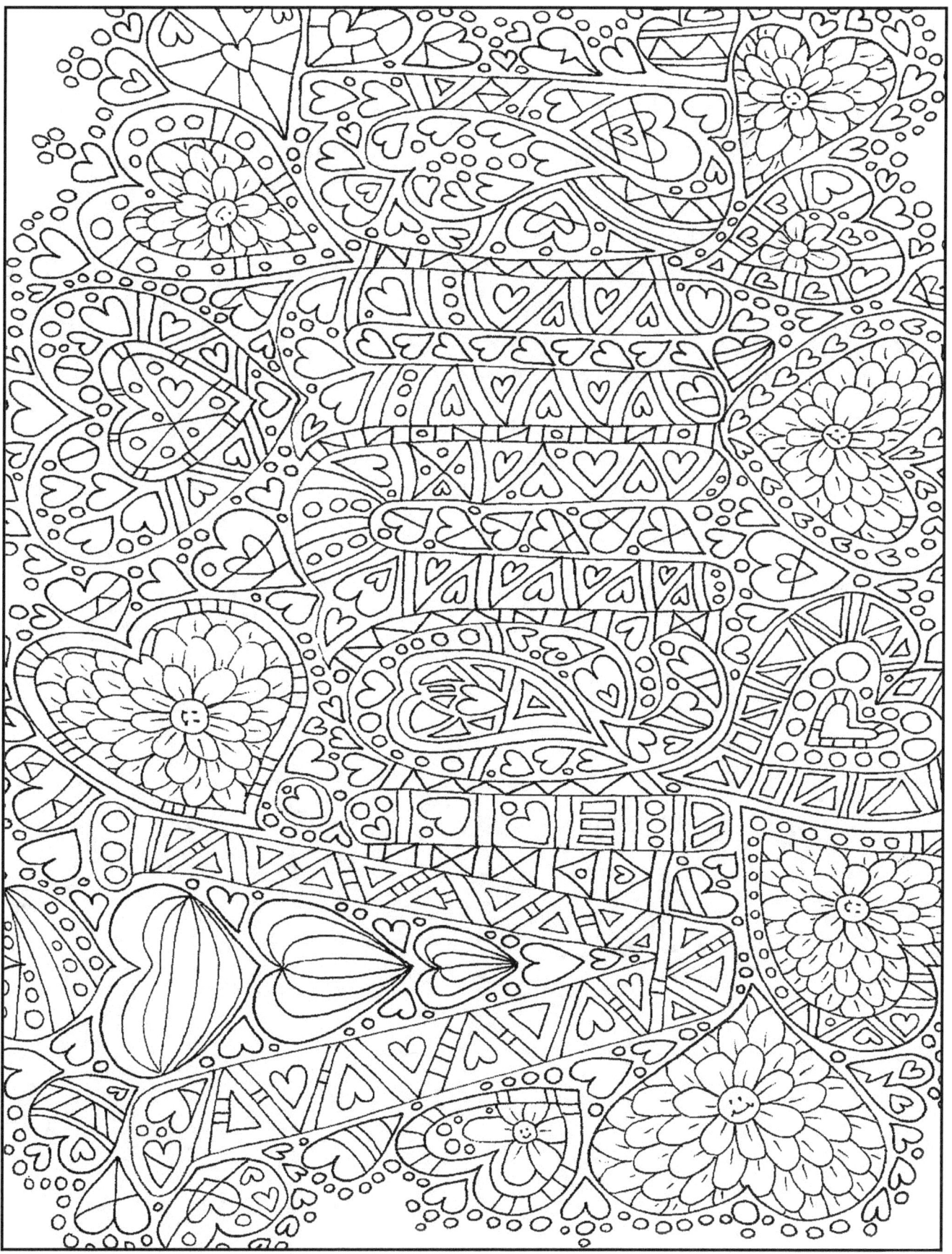

Check out other books by this author:

All books are available on Tamara's Amazon Author page at: https://www.amazon.com/Tamara-Kulish/e/B00IVWCAEI/

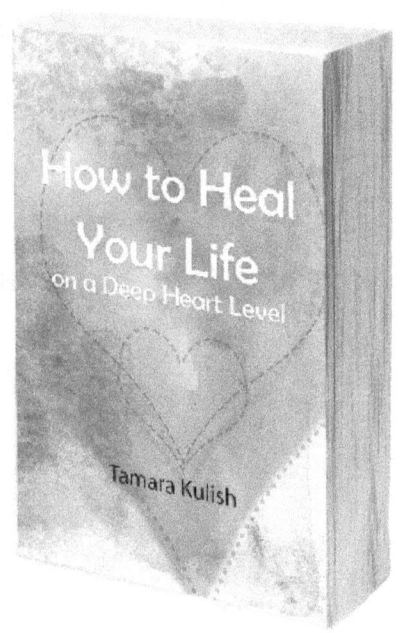
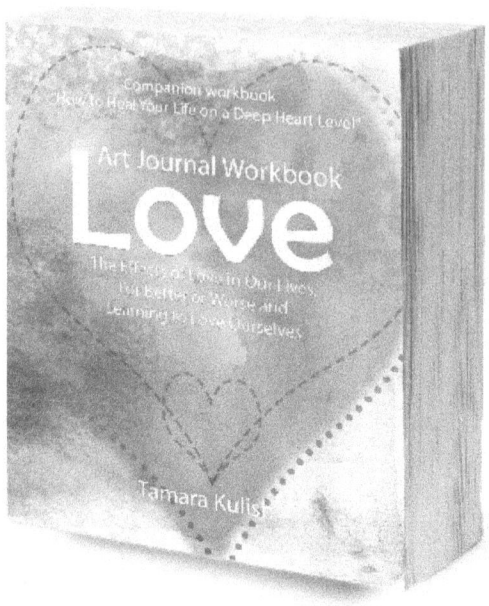
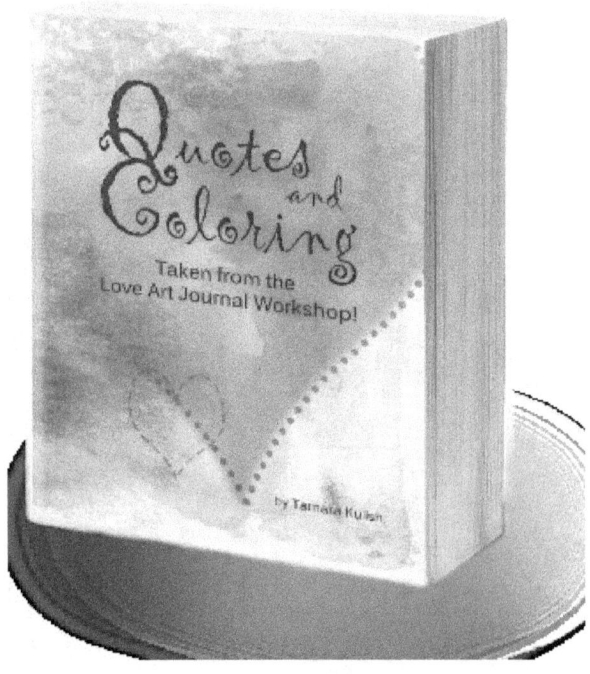

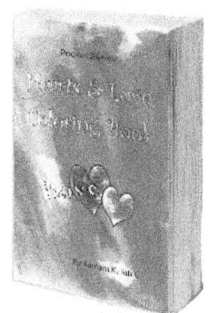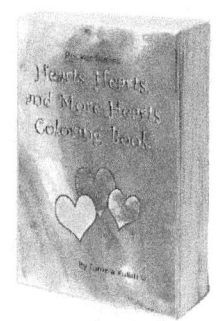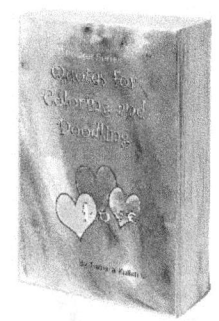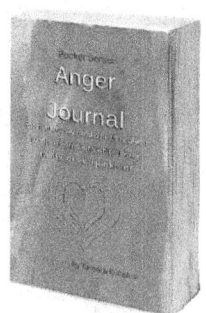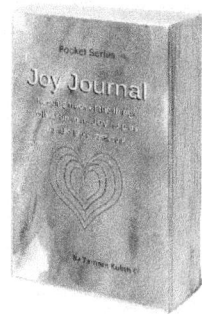

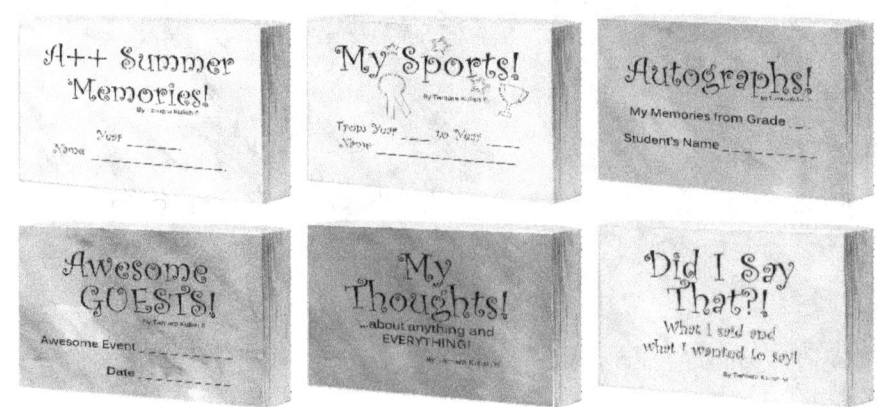

Thank you for buying
this book!

I hope you'll take the time to write a review... Other readers need to read your review!

www.ingramcontent.com/pod-product-compliance
Lightning Source LLC
Chambersburg PA
CBHW062216220526
45471CB00009B/3228